A SURVIVOR'S
GUIDE TO WASHINGTON

HOW TO SUCCEED WITHOUT LOSING YOUR SOUL

TORIE CLARKE

A SURVIVOR'S
GUIDE TO WASHINGTON

**HOW TO SUCCEED
WITHOUT LOSING
YOUR SOUL**

TORIE CLARKE

FOREWORD BY LEWIS BLACK
ILLUSTRATIONS BY NICK GALIFIANAKIS

To Dad, who knows more about
life, death and human nature
than anyone on the planet.

A Survivor's Guide to Washington
How to Succeed Without Losing Your Soul

Published by Voxie Media
Big Ideas. Short Books.™
voxiemedia.com

ISBN 978-0-9886203-6-0
eISBN 978-0-9886203-5-3

Printed in the United States of America
First Printing, 2014

Cover and interior design: Melanie Shellito of Artezen LLC
Proofreading: Alison Lueders of Great Green Content

ALSO BY TORIE CLARKE

*Lipstick on a Pig: Winning In the No-Spin Era
by Someone Who Knows the Game*

CONTENTS

FOREWORD

I can't think of anyone better to write a book about surviving (and even thriving!) in Washington D.C. than Torie Clarke, and I certainly wouldn't read one by anyone else. I wouldn't attempt to write one and I am from that area. (My book would be just one sentence: GET THE HELL OUT OF THERE NOW!)

I've known Torie forever—for so long that it would be ungentlemanly to tell you how long. We met because I was living with her sister, Caitlin, a wonderful actress. Even though Caitlin and I didn't marry, I always considered her folks to be the best in-laws I've ever known.

I met Torie when she was riding in a horse show on her way to not becoming an equestrian. She looked so natural in a riding outfit with a crop in her hand that I knew she was going to become a Republican. Some other tip-offs were that she was big on horse shows and called herself Torie (Tory).

Actually, that's not a fair joke, because she's a lot smarter than anyone who calls themselves either a Republican or a Democrat. The difference between the two parties is simple—the Democrats are dumb and the Republicans are stupid. Torie isn't dumb or stupid—she's ridiculously smart, but like both parties, she wasn't smart enough to leave Washington D.C. after she went to college there. (After growing up there, I fled at my first opportunity. That's how you know I'm smart.)

After I graduated from college, I lasted about nine months working for the federal government at the now defunct Appalachian Regional Commission. (It was an anti-poverty agency. Those are a few words you never hear anymore, now that we've cured poverty. But I digress.) After that experience I knew that I could never work in an office of any kind—be it business or government—and it destroyed any interest I might have had of getting into politics.

As someone who's made a very good living mocking politicians, I can tell you that you will never find a better book to help you deal with the idiots, jackasses and sociopaths who inhabit the halls of our government offices, and of offices across America. It also gives anyone who is dealing with the quagmire of partisan politics a clear road map to get through the muck without being swallowed up by it. (The savings on your dry-cleaning alone make this book a great investment.)

Even more amazing is that Torie has gathered great advice from all parts of the political spectrum. That is part of what gives her book clarity amidst what is normally chaos. This book is therefore not only about surviving the politics of the office but the politics of politics. And by answering the questions posed to her, she has given us a deeper understanding of the nuts and bolts of our democratic process.

From reading this book, I now understand quite clearly why I couldn't work in an office or be active in politics and why I had to leave D.C. What Torie handles with such great humor and grace would have driven me insane.

I have watched Torie for years as she has explained quite clearly to the world the behavior and decisions of ridiculously powerful men who couldn't explain their decisions or behavior. So pay attention—whether your cubicle is in the office of a small accounting firm in Peoria or just down the hall from a U.S. Senator. There is a path you can follow, and Victoria Clarke has shined a bright light on it so that you can find your way to success and maybe even happiness.

I'm glad I didn't read this book 30 years ago. I might never have left D.C.

— Lewis Black

INTRODUCTION

"Just Don't Embarrass Us"

A few years ago, my mother asked me to speak at the Women's Club in Sewickley, Pennsylvania, my hometown. Sewickley is a cute little town about 12 miles up the Ohio River from Pittsburgh. Some claim the unusual name meant "sweet water" to the local Native Americans, way back when. Depending on your historian, it could be a reference to the waters of the Ohio River, the syrup from the local maple trees or the Indians' homemade liquor.

With a population of about 3,900 people and one traffic light, Sewickley is not quite a Norman Rockwell painting, but it was an embarrassingly great place to be a kid. When I grew up there no one locked their doors, everybody knew everybody else, and the Sewickley Hotel, the only place in town with a liquor license, was where steelworkers coming off a night shift happily traded shots with college kids home for visits.

Founded in 1897, the Women's Club charter says its mission is "to unite the influence, sympathy and counsel of the women of Sewickley Valley and to promote legislative, educational, moral and social measures." Authors, birdwatchers, journalists, musicians and diplomats of varying degrees of success and fame share their stories in the Women's Club's esteemed Lecture Series. Being asked to speak there is a real honor if you're a native. And for most people, it's probably a fun thing to do—but not for me, because doing so would require me to speak in front of my parents.

Maybe it's leftover trauma from being the youngest of five girls, the four older ones being very smart and very successful in school and sports—which I was not. Whatever the reason, I cringed when my mother called and asked me to come up. Talk endlessly with reporters and editors? No problem. Live televised press briefings at the Pentagon? Done. A *60 Minutes* interview? Easy. Dueling with Jon Stewart on *The Daily Show*? Not easy, but I've done that too. But speaking in front of my parents? Terrifying.

But I had to say yes... and I spent the next several weeks regretting it.

The night before the speech, I was driving the 250 miles from my house in Chevy Chase to my parents' place in Sewickley. MapQuest says it should take close to five hours but no self-respecting Pittsburgher would consider anything over four hours, twenty minutes acceptable. Especially if you have made the drive as many times as I have. Hundreds of trips—visits from college, high school reunions, taking the kids to see their grandparents—have made the drive a familiar and—usually—comforting one for me.

Not this time. Neither the familiar landmarks nor the blaring radio could distract me from the growing sense of dread about my upcoming speech, which was scheduled for 10 the next morning. As I was taking the Monroeville exit to swing around downtown Pittsburgh—one of the greatest skylines anywhere, and yes I've been to Paris!—my cell phone rang. It was my Mom. Since it was close to 11 p.m., I knew it must be something important. It was. "Your father and I have just one favor to ask," she said. "Don't embarrass us tomorrow."

Ouch. In hindsight—and knowing that my mother was one of the kindest, most sensitive people not officially declared a saint—I think what she was really saying was: "Don't use any of that colorful language you sometimes employ." At that moment, though, waves of nausea washed over me as my now sweaty hands squeezed the wheel. *Why, oh why did I say yes?* I thought.

The next morning, I was practically vibrating with nervousness as my parents and I walked to the Edgeworth Club, which is more than 100 years old and the official "home" of the Women's Club events. The scene of many dances, wedding receptions and summer musicals, it is right out of *Dirty Dancing*. We spent a lot of time there as kids, and probably our all-time favorite activity was the Club's version of Bingo, which they called "EDGIO." It was great fun until the night one of the guests—just a wee bit over-served—stood on a table and declared proudly, "My name is Giovanni Edgio!" And that was the end of EDGIO.

Sadly for me, no alcohol would be served during my speech. That morning, the ballroom was filled with about 125 of Sewickley's finest—and oldest. My parents were in their early 80s then, and they were some of the youngest people in the room. There were walkers and IV bags on rolling poles, and oxygen tanks were tucked under several chairs. While I took my seat next to the podium, my parents found seats off to one side, near the front.

As everyone settled into their seats, a very sweet and tiny lady came up to me and clasped my hand. "I'm your introducer," she said, "and my grandson helped me get your government resume!" I was too nervous to fully process what she'd just said. Nor did I notice the large stack of papers in her arms. I should have. After the President of the Women's Club made her remarks and introduced the head of the Lecture Series, the head of the Lecture Series introduced my introducer as I felt flop-sweat starting to trickle down my back. Finally my tiny friend started in on her stack of papers, now placed carefully in front of her on the podium.

As most people know, when you take a high-level government job—as I have done, several times—the price of entry includes massive amounts of paperwork. To get the required security clearances you relinquish all notions of privacy and reveal every detail about your life, including any and all jobs you've had—starting with that lemonade stand in 2nd grade. Somehow the grandson had obtained the "work experience" section of one of my applications, and his grandmother proceeded to read it. Line by line. Word for word.

"Miss Clarke currently works for the Department of Defense, where she has been since May 19, 2001. Prior to that, she was the head of the Washington office of the international public relations firm Hill & Knowlton. She was there from 1999 until she went to the Pentagon."

As she kept talking I noticed that my right knee was bobbing up and down like a sewing machine.

"Prior to that she was the head of Bozell Eskew, an issues advocacy and image advertising firm. Before that, she was a Vice President of Public Affairs for the National Cable and Telecommunications Association in Washington D.C., where she worked from 1993 to 1998."

She kept going. She mentioned my brief stint at another public relations firm. She highlighted my time working for Senator John McCain. My job in the U.S. Trade Representative's office. Press Secretary for the 1992 Bush-Quayle presidential campaign. An internship in then-Vice President Bush's press office. A congressional campaign in Kansas. A stint at the Justice Department. "My god," I thought, "she's going to mention me pouring beers at Mitch's Tavern!"

After five minutes of this, my introducer was only about halfway through her stack of papers, but as she paused to catch her breath, a lady in the front row bellowed, "It sounds like that lady can't hold a job!" The crowd tried—and failed—to stifle laughter. And I don't care how old you are, if you're in trouble, and you have a parent nearby, you turn to them for help. I wheeled around and saw my folks nudge each other and murmur—I am sure—"We've been thinking that for a long time!"

And what could I say? I *have* had lots of jobs. The good news is that several of them were fantastic and even the worst one taught me something. I've met people from all over the world, from dentists to dictators, and I've learned something from every one of them, even those I despised. Washington D.C. is a mostly wonderful town filled with mostly wonderful people (mostly) trying to do a good job. And despite its reputation, I firmly believe it's a place where you can survive—even thrive—without selling your soul to the devil, or a cable-news segment producer.

So many young (and old!) people come to Washington because they want more than a job—they want to make a difference. And they need—and deserve—some help. Work in Washington long enough and you'll be asked to speak with someone new to town or a young person seeking career advice. They all ask the same question—"How do you get ahead?"— and I repeat the same advice and stories.

Be resilient. My childhood ambition to ride and train horses professionally fizzled out due to my less than exceptional talent and my less than unlimited funds. Then I thought I wanted to be a vet, but Organic Chemistry (in which I got a merciful "D") thought differently. I was on a clear path to be a staff photographer for the *Washington Star*—followed, I assumed, by a gig at *National Geographic*—when the *Star* folded.

Be willing to plunge into uncharted territory. Before working for then-Congressman John McCain of Arizona, I had been west of the Mississippi just once. Despite seldom traveling outside the country I went to work in the U.S. Trade Representative's office, and I had zero military experience when I went to work at the Pentagon.

Be comfortable with "No." In a society filled with "Yes" men and women shamelessly sucking up to their bosses, it's tempting to mouth the party line, and easy to believe that you need to get along to get ahead. Sometimes my greatest contribution has been my willingness to say to those in power, "You really don't want to hear this, but... "

The many jobs I've had and the many talented people I've worked with have filled me with good advice and even better stories. Some of them are funny, some are infuriating and many of them have a valuable lesson that will help you get ahead in Washington, or in Walla Walla. I've shared many of these stories with my dad, one of the very few people I know whose work—he's a doctor—is also his passion. "Write 'em down!" he'd say. "You'll forget 'em if you don't." And so I have.

If you're wondering how I came up with the questions for the book, they are all real. They're ones I've been asked at speaking events, at cocktail parties and via email.

A recurring theme in this book—and of living in D.C.—is the tension between doing well and doing good. I'm always trying to do both, and I know that I'm happiest when I'm helping others do better. With this book I hope to pass along some of the wisdom I've gained—accidentally or otherwise—over the years.

Even if I can't hold onto a job.

CHAPTER ONE

DOING WELL, DOING GOOD AND THE PROPER CARE AND FEEDING OF LEAKERS

"Do Something Before She Jumps Out The Window Naked!"

Q: Help! I'm trying to decide between a low-paying job with a congressman I admire versus better wages and hours at a public relations firm downtown. My sister says there's no "nobility" in PR, but nobility doesn't pay the bills, and my student loan debt could sink a third-world country. Is it possible to do well in Washington D.C. and do good?

A: Thanks for getting the most important career question out of the way first. Doing well and doing good aren't mutually exclusive—even at a PR firm, despite what your sister says. And nobody says you have to do one or the other—I've happily made a career of having many careers, and every job helped me in the next one.

If you're relatively young and not yet worried about paying for braces for your kids and the family dog, get some public sector experience. A big selling point for the Hill is that a young person there can have responsibility way beyond what he'd be handed in the private sector. Work hard, keep your nose and shirt clean and

in short order you can help draft and pass legislation. Sign on to a
bank, say, and you'll likely spend several years working your way up
from flunky to chief flunky. Down the road, potential employers
will value what you learned on the Hill, despite congressional
approval ratings in the single digits.

Now let's talk about PR firms. They drove U.S. automakers
down the path to better fuel efficiency and performance. They
nudged pharmaceutical manufacturers to spend more on research
and insurance companies to be more transparent in their claims
process. They helped the U.S. Treasury create the 50 State Quarter
program, one of the most successful "collectibles" ever. Not every
client is about curing cancer, but that's okay. Often the PR firm's
role is to deliver the bad news, convincing the client to do the right
thing even if it's painful and costly. The PR firm is the one who tells
the client: "You have a crazy aunt in the attic, and you have to do
something about her before she jumps out the window naked."

Most firms have fairly high standards about which clients they
will take. It's not (this will shock your sister) always about defending
third-world dictators or helping cigarette companies brainwash
kids with comic books. And in controversial areas (e.g., you're pro-
life and your firm is helping Planned Parenthood), most allow you
to opt out of an account if you have moral objections. Of course, if
you opt out too often you probably landed in the wrong firm and
should opt out permanently and get another job.

Your dilemma goes to the heart of the "What should I do with
my life?" question so many people ask when considering a job in
Washington. My friend Mary Matalin is a Republican strategist,
political genius, devoted mom and the most loyal of buddies. She
also has an enviable gift for cutting through the crap.

"Don't even think about working in Washington D.C. unless

you absolutely believe doing good *is* doing well," Mary says. "The professionals who end up making a good living in policy and politics here worked long and hard hours for low wages for an indeterminate time, proving their abilities, gaining experience and building relationships, which are the essential lubrication of one-industry D.C. "The personal rocket fuel of political work is a core belief system, a philosophical allegiance and coherent worldview. The rewards of the work are the furtherance of that belief system, the collection of unique memories and the camaraderie of life-long foxhole buddies; in short, the real stuff of life that money can't buy. At some point, the skills, experience and relationships coalesce to provide a living wage that allows you to move out of the group house and consume more than just ciggies and red wine."

I warned you that Mary's blunt, and brilliant. I wouldn't trade my six years on Capitol Hill for all the ciggies in China. And washing dishes on the weekends at Brooke Rental in Vienna, Virginia was a small price to pay to make ends meet on a congressional salary.

My advice: Go for the Hill job, and you'll never regret it.

Q: I'm working on a losing campaign in which neither the candidate nor the campaign manager has a clue. Recently, several people in our District were killed during a gang fight, including a 16-year-old who was just in the wrong place at the wrong time. Our candidate refuses to comment, not even a generic sympathetic statement about the 'tragic loss of life.' He's afraid he'll get drawn into a debate about gun control, which our opponent supports. I'm considering a few strategic leaks and anonymous tweets to get my point across. It might help and, at the very least, maybe I'll save my reputation.

A: Danger! Danger! Immediately step away from Twitter! Taking shots from within would be reputation suicide. You are delusional if you think colleagues won't smoke out the anonymous whiner. Remember long-time Washington pundit Joe Klein's "anonymous" authorship of *Primary Colors*, the thinly veiled novel about Bill Clinton? Klein was outed in a few weeks. We all have a unique way of speaking and writing, and you're probably no different. More important, it's the wrong thing to do. There's no easier way to get attention than to "pee in your own nest," but that doesn't make it right. The reputations that soar (and last the longest) in Washington are those built on hard work, honesty and loyalty.

If you are as good at your job as you think you are, you should be able to persuade your colleagues, campaign manager and candidate to take a stand. And if they still won't listen, then you have an easy decision to make: suck it up or pack it up. Once you resign, you can criticize all you want.

Donna Brazile is a veteran political strategist who's worked on many Democratic campaigns, including running Vice President Gore's presidential bid in 2000. She has friends and fans from the far left to the far right. (I call her the Green Room Fairy Godmother because every makeup person in town adores her and that's where she dispenses sound advice on everything from sore throats to love affairs to the best chili recipe.) She sympathizes with your frustration.

"On numerous occasions, I have tried to stop a candidate from going down in flames," Donna says. "It's difficult to shut up or step aside when you feel passionate about a candidate or cause, but don't be reckless and try to stop a moving train from reaching its destination, or save a freefalling candidate who won't accept your parachute."

I know a little bit about floundering. When the Bush-Quayle '92 campaign dragged me into service as its press secretary, I had a great job—working for Carla Hills in the U.S. Trade Representative's office—and no desire to leave. When I finally decided to take the new job, my rationalization was that I would be working with the best of the best in the campaign world, and I would learn so much from them.

What I learned was how to get your head kicked during a national election. For starters, we had three campaign managers, and our campaign motto should have been "Who's In Charge?" All three had impressive resumes and an admirable devotion to President Bush. And it wasn't that they fought over turf. Just the opposite—they were all too nice, careful not to offend one another or the White House staff.

Our campaign went into a steep dive early and never pulled up. We started campaigning too late, we zigged on the economy when we should have zagged, and we couldn't believe that a "draft-dodging, pot smoking, skirt-chasing guy from Arkansas" was eating our lunch. In a word, we sucked. As the year wore on, our casual friends abandoned the campaign and started carping. Then many of our good friends stopped campaigning for us, and didn't return our phone calls. But they happily returned calls from the media and regaled them with lots of "*This* is what they're doing wrong... " stories. Some put their names to their quotes and some didn't.

By September, not a day went by that some reporter didn't implore me to dish. "Look, Torie," they'd say, "Someone right down the hall from you spent an hour with me this morning. I have a good sense of what's going on; I just want you to fill in some of the details. You can do it on any basis you want." That's code for "stab somebody in the back, and we won't put your name on it."

By October my good friends were offering their condolences and suggesting that I start my personal career rehabilitation by helping some of those reporters. "Let them know that you get it, Torie," they'd say. "You want to work in this town again." But by

November, I wasn't so sure I ever wanted to work in this town again. I seldom say, "I am so proud that I… " It's not how I was raised. Plus, I just don't have that much to boast about. I am proud, though, that I didn't trash anybody on that campaign. It would have been easy, and it would have made me feel better—briefly. But after a couple of days, I would have hated myself.

A few weeks after the election I got a handwritten note from soon-to-be former President Bush, which made it clear he knew that I had not sold him out. "You stayed in there with me, shoulder to shoulder, never jumping sideways when the going got tough. You certainly had, have, always will have my respect and appreciation."

Mary—as always—puts this issue into focus more succinctly: "The first thing you need to do is get a pack of Marlboro Lights and a basic cabernet or any *not*-low-calorie six-pack and sit down by the Tidal Basin at dusk and ask yourself, *How did I end up with a clueless candidate?*

"If you hope to be happy and successful in the political business, you will have figured out (before you start working on a wine-and-ciggie headache) that worrying about your reputation is the absolute worst thing you can do. Your labor and loyalty belong to your candidate and the home team. If you can't live by that code, get out *now*! There are plenty of dog-eat-dog, me-first professions in which you can excel. If you want to be a true-blue political warrior and you have somehow ended up with Candidate Clueless, you have two honorable courses of action: salute smartly and soldier on, or quit. In either case, shut up!"

Other than the part about sucking on Marlboro Lights, I'm in total agreement with Mary. Agree or disagree with your candidate, it is his campaign. It's your job to offer your advice—repeatedly, if necessary—and remain loyal to the no-doubt bitter end.

Q: A cable news network wants to hire me as a talking head to side with the Obama Administration in debates. Is it unethical to accept that gig if I sometimes think the President is way off base?

A: First, some crucial advice about doing work for cable news: Don't get attached to any executive, producer or booker. They come and go so often it's like having goldfish. Just when you get to know them and name them and buy them cute scuba divers for their bowls, they die and you're flushing them down the toilet. Or in the case of execs, producers and bookers, they swim to another network.

Now back to your question: Unless they're complete idiots they won't expect you to be in lockstep with the President. And disagreeing occasionally should enhance your credibility. But don't kid yourself. Media, especially television, want people to take strident views and engage in polarizing arguments. When I first signed with CNN to be one of their talking heads for a presidential election, I believed the execs who told me they welcomed my even-handed approach. Hah! Throughout the year some sweet young thing would call me an hour or two before we were going to tape a segment and say, "I just wanted to check in and make sure you and Democratic operative X disagree, so can I ask you a few questions?" I'd answer honestly, the assistant would usually mutter a few confused "Okay's" and sign off.

I tried and failed to play the part they wanted me to play. I found it hard to slash and burn. I wanted to discuss, not argue. Some people are great at it. Paul Begala, Clinton guru and brilliant political operative, feeds the cable beast as well as anyone I know. Although I sometimes accused him of hiring a joke writer, I know his witty responses and cutting jibes come naturally to him. Even he could take it too far, though. Once, in a moderately heated debate about Iraq on CNN, Paul compared four top Bush Administration officials to strains of venereal disease. He even had the scientific names!

Short answer: When in doubt, tell the truth—to the network heads who want to hire you and to the people listening to you when you're on air. You and the network will be more credible in the long run.

Q: After six years of grunt jobs in congressional offices and one stint as press secretary for a House member, I'm the press secretary for a Senate committee. Until now, no one's cared what I— or my boss—had to say about anything. Now we're in demand, and I'm confused about the unwritten rules of dealing with the media. Our chief of staff says I have to be more strategic and use leaks to better manage our news coverage. When is it okay to leak, and when isn't it?

A: To leak or not to leak? That is the question that often creates Shakespearean dramas in Washington. Leaks can be useful, but they're best executed by people with years of experience, and given to members of the media who are known and trusted. Leaks can get your communications on offense, always a good thing, but use them improperly, and you risk lowering your credibility, and that of your boss.

There are no "Leaks 101" college courses (yet), but there are people who have worked in government and journalism who have a keen sense of the "beauty and beast" of leaking. Pete Williams, currently the top NBC correspondent covering the Supreme Court and the Department of Justice, got his start in radio in his home state of Wyoming. He became then-Congressman Dick Cheney's press secretary, and when Cheney was tapped by President Bush to be Secretary of Defense, Pete went to the Pentagon as the Assistant Secretary of Defense. He has an acute sense of the potential value of leaks and some solid guidelines for gauging when they are a good idea.

"It's your boss's decision," Pete says. "If he or she tells you not to leak something, that's that. And it's never okay to leak classified information, because that's a crime. But beyond those shoals lies a vast sea of leaking, without which Washington's daily information exchange would dry up.

"A leak might be a tip about what a government report is going to say, who's going to testify before a high-profile hearing or what committee investigators are discovering. On the most principled end of the scale, government officials leak to make things public that they think people should know. In the middle are leaks to further an agenda. On the other end are leaks that put political opponents in a less favorable light.

"If you think a leak would help your boss or be in the public interest, then go ahead. You'll be doing what all your congressional colleagues are already doing. In fact, there are times when a failure to leak something puts you behind the curve, and on the defensive. Sometimes it's better to do it without asking the boss, who can then remain above the fray, but if you are seriously in doubt, ask."

Let me emphasize one of his points: It's never okay to leak classified information. That could be jail time. No matter how trivial the information (that probably shouldn't have been classified in the first place), don't do it!

Q: How do you keep your ego in check when you work at high levels of government or corporate America?

A: This takes care of itself most of the time. This town has a way of humbling those it once elevated and piercing the bubbles of celebrity that accompany high-profile jobs. Just when you think you are really hot stuff, somebody dumps a bucket of shaved ice in your underwear.

I've appeared on all the news networks, broadcast and cable, talking about everything from national security to politics to Michael Jackson (somehow there was a Washington connection). Often people bump into me on the street and say "Hey, I saw you on CNN last night." As a joke I always ask them what I talked about. They can rarely remember, but often say, "I don't know, but you looked great," or, more often, "I don't know, but I hated your outfit."

Talking-head stuff is a little like fortune cookie predictions—it all sounds pretty good when you first say it or hear it, but an hour later you can't remember a bit of it.

Our youngest son Charlie understands that better than most. At a party at our house, a woman was being nice to Charlie (a good idea) and patronizing him in that way some older people try to manage small children (a bad idea). Charlie was six, but he was tough.

"So I often see your mommy on TV," she said sweetly.

"Yeah?" Charlie grumbled back, barely disguising his boredom.

"Tell me, Charlie," she said, "what does your mommy talk about when she's on TV?"

Looking her dead in the eyes, Charlie responded with wisdom beyond his years: "Blah, blah, blah, blah, blah blah... "

SHE DOES THIS BEFORE ALL
HER MEDIA APPEARANCES.

CHAPTER TWO

WALKING THE WORK/LIFE HIGH WIRE WITHOUT FALLING OFF

"Only Once Did We Lose Charlie in Baggage Claim"

Q: I am a legislative assistant in a Senate office filled with hard workers and one out-of-control sycophant who drives the rest of us crazy. He sends countless texts to our boss, often at 3 a.m., just to show how hard he's working. He chirps "You are absolutely right!" every time the Senator speaks, even if it's just to order a sandwich. After a recent press conference (not the Senator's best performance), Bobby Brown-noser was high–fiving him! Sadly, his efforts seem to be effective. The Senator gives him lots of "Attaboys!" and often implies that the rest of us don't work as hard. We all work hard, but we'd like to have lives, too, and some self-respect.

A: Sycophants are as common in Washington as dead potted plants. Every office has at least one. One of the worst I encountered was at the Pentagon, where you want smart and talented people, not parrots. We called him "Ed McMahon" behind his back because, like the old late-night television host Johnny Carson's sidekick, he regularly boomed "You are correct, sir!" whenever Secretary of Defense Donald Rumsfeld said something.

I share your contempt for brown-nosers and will raise you one: They're often the best at *looking* productive when, in reality, they *produce* the least. I call them mattress mice. They scurry around looking busy, but all they really do is leave droppings on your desk and contribute nothing of significance. In the dark ages, when suck-ups had to write things down on paper, John McCain's office had one who would leave his memos on the senator's chair with the time written in the corner—10:20 p.m. or 1:15 a.m.—so when John came in the next morning he would see how hard the fellow was working. A few of us who lived nearby retaliated by sneaking in late at night to scratch out the original time or change the PM to AM.

That kind of revenge is hard to pull off in the digital age, so you may have to a) accept that brown-nosers are part of life; and b) resort to more mature and direct action to shame the knucklehead. Talk to your boss about it—privately. He may not even be aware of what's going on. Who wouldn't want to be fawned over and praised 30 times a day? Don't use the entire conversation to trash your colleague—no matter how much he may deserve it—and give specific examples. At the very least, you'll sensitize your boss to the issue. And I'm betting (maybe I'm hoping here?) he tells you he values substance over sucking up.

Q: I have a fairly normal job by Washington standards, which means private-sector with 10-hour days and few weekends on call. As a senior political appointee, my wife is on call (and on Facebook and Twitter) 24/7. Since her job is more important than mine, she expects me to run the household, including cleaning, grocery shopping and booking play dates. I get it—she's saving the world, and I'm just trying to save my sanity and oft-neglected job—but does that sound remotely fair to you?

A: Fair? That depends on the chat you and your wife had before she took that job. It's fair if you hashed it out over a bottle wine; unfair if she blind-sided you. When I was approached about working at the Pentagon, I repeatedly assured my husband, Brian, that I had no interest in the job. "I'm the head of the "Friends Don't Let Friends Go Back Into Government" Committee," I'd remind friends who'd heard rumors.

I forgot to tell Brian when I changed my mind. My bad. Worse, he found out by reading about it in the *Washington Post*. Oops. Once we got past that communications error, we had several lengthy talks about what the job would mean for us, and our young children. We agreed that Brian would have to assume many more responsibilities on the home front. His work in finance and housing would take a hit.

I got to be a 1960s suburban Dad! Go to work and rarely check in during the day. Come home late, 8:30 on a good night, and Brian has fed the kids, helped one with an overdue science fair project, bathed them and put them in PJs. The kids are thrilled to see me, mostly because I wasn't the one nagging them during the day. I'd read them a few stories and tuck them in bed. Being a 1960s suburban Dad can be very easy. Look at Don Draper.

You have to know your role and always remember who's in charge. The wife of a longtime Admiral once told me to imagine the Navy spouse often deployed for several months. "I'm Commander in Chief on the home front," she said. "And he can't get in my chain of command from ten thousand miles away or even when he's home on leave." It took me awhile to learn that lesson.

You and your spouse also need to coordinate your movements like an invading army. Several times Brian and I found ourselves doing a kid handoff at National Airport as one of us headed out of town as the other was coming in. Only once did we lose Charlie in Baggage Claim.

It's also paramount that you get help. If you can't afford an au pair, maybe a neighborhood teenager can help out after school. Convince a grandparent to pitch in. And know that the person caring for your babies is the most important person in the world. Pay as much as you can and bring home fabulous gifts from Kabul. Missed your spouse's birthday? No worries, but don't forget the babysitter's. That is the most important person in your life right now.

ABC's hardest-working man is George Stephanopoulos, who co-hosts *Good Morning America*, fills in often on the *ABC Evening News* and leads *This Week* on Sunday mornings. His wife, Ali Wentworth, is no slouch in the work department, either—she's a successful actress, TV host and author. They live in New York City with their two young daughters and balance the work/life issues as well as any couple I know. George says he relies on the same preparation and flexibility that help him thrive at work to meet the challenges of family life, including those times when both parents have unbreakable commitments on the night of the school play.

"You might be surprised at how rarely you face that kind of dilemma," he says. "If you plan ahead—and share work schedules early and often—most conflicts can be avoided with small adjustments. Take turns when necessary. Even when the conflict can't be planned away, reschedule that parent-teacher conference. Most teachers will understand. If they don't, it's not a crime to miss it just this once. Now the school play that your daughter sweated over for months? That's a different story. One of you has to be there. Absolutely. Positively. Then email a video to the traveler."

George's advice is perfect. Plan ahead and know that no one event is the end of the world. Most important, have a sense of humor. You'll be horrified when that baby's screaming in the background as you lead an agency conference call, but years later you'll laugh about it.

It takes a village to raise a kid, but it takes a mid-size city to help a family manage when one parent has a big Washington job.

Q: The third time my kids stole my iPhone I realized work was bleeding too much into my home life. The first two times we just chased them down and forced them to hand it over. They're getting bigger and smarter, though, and this time they hid it under the dog's bed, where it ran out of juice and was very hard to find. When is it okay to bring work home? In today's "always on" mentality, it's hard to go off the grid and still be considered relevant at work.

A: A kidnapped iPhone is a good sign that work has taken over your life. So is having your kid flush your passport down the toilet.

Regardless of how much work you have, you must set boundaries on how and when you are plugged in. For inspiration, get William Powers' book, *Hamlet's Blackberry: A Practical Philosophy for Building a Good Life in the Digital Age.* His family does a "digital purge" each week, unplugging all devices from sundown Friday to sunrise Monday. My favorite recommendation of his is to create "Walden Zones" in your home where no screens are permitted. Give your brain (and your loved ones) a break from beeps and buzzes and flashing lights.

Not everyone can have Walden Zones, but you can still bring some discipline to your digital doings. Stephanopoulos has to be "on" all the time, but he manages it brilliantly.

"I love my job," he says. "But there's a catch—I have to be reachable 24/7. That means my iPhone is always on. But having it in my pocket at home sure beats being at the office. What I have to work on is keeping it in my pocket until there's a real emergency. All it takes is willpower."

If you're George or are running the CIA, you and your family need to just accept that you're "always on" and will be getting texts at 3 a.m. But most of us just aren't that vital, and there are ways to go on a digital diet without sacrificing quality work. For starters, just say no. Or at least "not now." When you head home, put an auto-reply on your devices: "I currently have limited access to email and texts. If this is urgent, please call my cell or home number." That can dramatically cut back on the flood of incoming and you can focus on important things, like your kid's diorama of the Coliseum.

Chances are your work will influence your family, even if you think you left it at the office. In the weeks after 9/11, I didn't often talk about Osama Bin Laden at home (okay, not much), but our son Colin knew he was the number one bad guy. Colin was six years old then and had a sense of what happened that day.

One night I came home late from the Pentagon to find some drawings by the kids on the kitchen counter. Sipping the glass of wine Brian had thoughtfully left for me, I flipped through them. Devan's and Charlie's were mostly fish and ponies and ducks. Colin's was a little harder to figure out. There was something in the sky—a plane, maybe?—and a big pile of something on the ground—rocks? Falling from the plane were smaller rocks, and buried under the pile were two legs and little shoes sticking out. I couldn't remember the last time we had watched *The Wizard of Oz*, but his drawing looked like a weird version of the house falling on that wicked witch.

Several days later, Colin came home with another version of the same thing. Plane, little rocks falling on the big rocks under which there were legs and shoes. A few days later, another version, this time with more small rocks falling from the plane. Despite being an idiot, I realized Colin was trying to tell us something, so I asked him about his drawing as I put it on the fridge.

"You mean you can't tell?" he said, incredulous. "It's American planes dropping bombs on Osama Bin Laden!" A light bulb went on over my head—this must be Colin's way of dealing with his fears.

I made an appointment and went in to see his teacher, carrying several versions of "I want to kill a terrorist" in a yellow folder. My mind ranged over the possibilities: Maybe he's afraid? Overly aggressive? Was this a sign of deviant behavior caused, no doubt, by my bad parenting?

His teacher looked at each drawing carefully. "He's consistent, isn't he?"

"Yes," I said, "but is it something we need to worry about?"

His teacher slowly said, "I don't think so..."—as I breathed a huge sigh of relief—"Unless of course...." Her voice trailed off.

"Unless what?" I said, now worried.

"Unless," she laughed, "he starts putting *you* at the bottom of the pile!"

Q: The good news is that I have a high-level job in the Administration. I worked for years to get this job, toiling away in two Congressional offices as a legislative assistant, running errands for a mid-level bureaucrat in an agency. I finally got the job I've always wanted and thought I had it made. Now I'm not so sure. I never sleep, I grind my teeth, and I have no social life. Is the fame and glory of my job worth all that?

A: Wow. If I had such a high opinion of myself I'd probably not sleep either.

Just kidding. (Or not.) First of all, get some perspective. You are not alone—sleep deprivation and teeth-grinding are SOP in high-level jobs. As Nigel in *The Devil Wears Prada* says to a stressed out Andy: "Let me know when your personal life goes completely up in smoke. Then I'll know you're ready for a promotion."

Your question worries me for another reason. Did you take that job for the fame and glory? If so, you're about to get a pie in the face. For every person who says something nice about you there will be one or two who hate your guts.

And that's a price worth paying if you went into government for the right reasons. Do you want to make a difference in the policy arena? Do you want to help constituents back home who deserve a more effective federal government? If not, start packing.

Before you take these sorts of jobs, you have to weigh all the factors. Will your contributions, even if they're not perfect, outweigh the sacrifices you and your family will have to make? I left a cushy job and lifestyle to work at the Pentagon because I thought I could help haul the Department of Defense public affairs efforts into the 21st century. Although I didn't anticipate 9/11 or two wars, I knew the job wouldn't be easy.

But let's assume you are a *Mr. Smith Goes to Washington* kind of guy, and you're in it for the right reasons. These jobs can be grueling, mentally and physically. Take care of yourself so you can sleep at night and be at your best when your colleagues need you.

Ironically, I learned that lesson during one of the most stressful times in our country's history. Just a few short weeks after 9/11 we found ourselves in the midst of a mini-scandal because some knuckleheads had decided to call the military operations in Afghanistan "Infinite Justice." That name turned out to be very finite, as Muslims around the world told us how insulting it was to suggest that we, rather than Allah, would decide infinite justice for anyone. So the military wordsmiths went back to the drawing board. They swore they used computers and algorithms and such stuff. I'm pretty sure they scrawled words on a white board and threw darts until they came up with Operation Enduring Freedom. I drew the short straw one early Sunday morning and had to make sure the White House—

confident of our abilities on the battlefield but a lot less sure about our wordsmithing—was okay with the new name.

Through the White House communications center, I dialed up Karen Hughes, White House Communications head. "She's at church and asked not to be interrupted until later this morning, ma'am," a cheerful operator told me. An hour or so later Karen signed off on the new name and asked me to call National Security Advisor Condoleeza Rice, who was at Camp David. "She's working out, ma'am," the next operator told me. And when I did talk with her, Rice told me she wanted to run it by the President, but he was having lunch.

"*Hmmmm....,*" I thought. "I haven't been to church, worked out or sat down to a proper meal since 9/11. What is wrong with this picture?" Everything. They were right, and I was wrong. Sleep-deprived and jacked-up on caffeine and junk food is not the way to do your best.

So carve out time—even a little—for yourself and your sanity. Remind yourself that if the President of the United States has time to watch movies and play golf and hang with his family—which they all do—then you can. You'll be a lot more productive, and your teeth will thank you.

Q: I worked on the Hill for several years and had a low-level agency job before I left for the private sector. Now I'm back in government as an Undersecretary. Before, reporters were happy to talk with me about legislation or Administration policies. Now they're more interested in my personal life (I'm getting divorced) or my bank account (I worked for a health care firm that collapsed after I left). A reporter is working on a piece about my summer vacation on Martha's Vineyard. Shouldn't my personal life be off-limits?

A: There is a really easy solution here: Quit. Seriously. Being in the spotlight—which includes having reporters dig around in your personal life—comes with a high-level career.

Some things are off-limits—kids, for example. You and just about everybody else in town chose this life; your kids did not, and should not have to suffer because of your choices. But the good old days when newspapers didn't show pictures of FDR in a wheelchair are gone. Chances are your dinner at Equinox with your wife could get a mention on some blog, so tip well—the Twitterati will make sure everyone hears about it if you stiffed the waiter.

Behave yourself at your kid's soccer game. If you scream obscenities at the ref—no matter how deserved they might be—you'll be in the *Huffington Post* in minutes. Your schedule frees up and you hit the golf course? Don't cheat. Presidents get mulligans; Under-Secretaries do not.

Those are the easy examples, but there are serious considerations, too. Stick around long enough and you will get dragged into unpleasant situations—the inevitable Congressional investigations, the accusations of wrong-doing that may have no merit but do have political currency. Look up former Secretary of Labor Raymond Donovan, whose life and reputation were incinerated in a highly publicized scandal. When he was acquitted after months of scrutiny and many thousands of dollars in legal fees, Donovan said, "Which office do I go to, to get my reputation back?"

It's not right, it's not fair—it just is. So you have an easy choice. Accept it as yet another sacrifice you make for public service (including the vow of poverty and the sleep deprivation) and suck it up. Or step aside and let someone else take the abuse.

Q: From the time I was in 2nd grade, I planned to run for public office. I was Student Council President in high school, ran Young Democrats in college and volunteered on several campaigns. For nearly a decade I served on non-paying town councils, thinking it would help my chances when I did run for office. Along the way, I fell in love, got married, and became a father. Now I'm having second thoughts. What about the scrutiny my wife and kids will have to endure? I can handle seeing my life and career put under an electron microscope, but I don't want them to endure that kind of scrutiny. As my kids get older, will they have to defend my vote on a controversial issue when it comes up in debate class? Should my wife have to worry about some nut shooting up the Rayburn House Office Building?

A: That's a tough one. I've always felt bad for the spouses and families of public officials. It's rough enough if your wife/husband/mother/father is gone all the time, toiling away at the office or hitting every rubber-chicken event in the District. It's even worse when the work starts hurting the family's life.

Brian and I wanted our kids to understand and appreciate my job at the Pentagon, but we worried about them being in the spotlight. We wanted them to attend the Memorial Day ceremony at Arlington, but we didn't want the *Washington Post* to mention their names and ages, or where we lived.

Manage your expectations. You can only protect them so much, and there will occasionally be collateral damage. Be reasonable. No one should report on your son's visit to the orthodontist, but if your wife joins a protest in front of the Supreme Court, she's going to be in the papers.

And don't make a bad situation worse. If your daughter gets caught smoking pot, do not (as one former very senior Administration officials did) call news organizations and ask them not to report the story. If asked about it, you or your press secretary should say, "It's a family matter, and we have no comment." The millions of parents who've gone through something similar will support you completely.

And there's a tragic edge to this dilemma. As former Congresswoman Gabby Giffords and 20 other people tragically found out in 2011 at a shopping center in Tucson, Arizona, there are crazies out there, some of whom have it in for public officials and those around them.

My father was too kind to ever tell me, but when I was at the Pentagon he worried day and night that some psycho would get aggravated by an assertive woman waging an information war with Al Qaeda and take a shot at me. Only after I left the Pentagon did he tell me how glad he was that I got out of there alive.

MY WORK-LIFE BALANCE IMPROVED
IMMEDIATELY WHEN I STOPPED
TALKING ABOUT MY WORK-LIFE BALANCE.

CHAPTER THREE

WAR STORIES OF BEING A WOMAN IN A MAN'S WORLD

"Rode Hard and Put Up Wet"

Q: I'm about to take a job at a place where the entire senior management team is male. They wear boots to work, are in fantasy football leagues and loudly discuss their love-hate fantasies about Angelina Jolie. My boots are Jimmy Choo's and the last league I was in was Junior... Am I nuts?

A: You're not nuts... unless you took the job because it seemed like a great way to meet guys. But ask yourself a few questions before you unpack your boxes. Do you like the stated mission of the place? Whether it's widgets or weapons, you should have more than a passing interest in what they're selling/making/unloading. You'll be spending 10 to 12 hours a day with your colleagues, and since they probably won't share your love of Louboutins, you'll have to find other common ground.

Do you have a sense of humor? If you do your job well the "guys" will probably focus more on your work than your gender. And while some behavior is appropriate only in a locker room, you may soon be treated like one of the guys, with all the ribald jokes that go with that status.

And ask yourself a question about the people with whom you'll work. Did they hire you because they needed to diversify their senior ranks? If so, do you mind being a token? I was offended when some said I got my job in the male-dominated Pentagon because I wore skirts—but no Louboutins (too rich for my shoe-tree).

Based on my pre-hire interview with Defense Secretary Donald Rumsfeld and several conversations we had after I signed on, I knew he hired me for the same reason he hired most of his senior staff. He wanted people unafraid of change with the guts to haul the antiquated defense bureaucracy into the 21st century. And while some thought putting a person with no military experience in my job was insane, I knew it was a smart move on a few levels. The Pentagon didn't need yet another military expert—it needed someone who could help explain the military's new mission to a public largely unaware of what our country's men and women in uniform were up to.

Weekly Standard writer Fred Barnes disagreed. A few weeks after my nomination was announced, he wrote an article entitled, *The Bush Quotas—Now Look Who's Counting by Race and Gender*. In it, he declared that my selection was "to comply with the White House's insistence on women or minorities in high positions." Fred's horse in this race was Tom DeFrank, a veteran journalist with a military background. As Fred and Tom both know, Don Rumsfeld rarely does something because of someone else's agenda.

The good news is that once you're doing a job like the one I took at the Pentagon, you are insanely busy. I think someone told me about Fred's piece, but I didn't have time to read it until years later.

Q: I'm the Executive Assistant to a department head in a government agency. He is a terrible sexist who has surrounded himself with men who were either in his fraternity, went to the same high school or played lacrosse, as he did. He is really good at covering his tracks. He's very careful about what he puts in emails and makes sure there are no witnesses when he says inappropriate things to me about my clothes, my tan and my boyfriend. He often refers to one of his female colleagues as a "fat ass" or "battle axe" and says she has "permanent PMS." I'm sick of it—I've lined up another job and will be giving notice shortly. My gut tells me I should blow the whistle on him before I go, but my practical side tells me not to burn bridges. Should I at least warn whomever he chooses to replace me? Also (and I know this is none of my business), he gets a credit card bill sent to the office—obviously to avoid his wife's scrutiny—and I saw a charge to an escort service.

A: Your practical side? Why are you worried about burning bridges with this bum? Run, do not walk, to your Human Resources Department and burn *him*. Give them facts, not feelings. That kind of behavior is never acceptable, but I think it's even more appalling when the offender's paycheck comes from the American taxpayers. Respect the office in which you get to work and do your best to protect it, even if it's only in your final two weeks on the job. You have a chance to do that by taking this clown down.

Q: I went to an all girls' school, primarily because my parents thought I would get leadership experience running things (e.g. student council, the newspaper) that I might not get at a co-ed school. I worked at American Express because it's regularly named one of the best companies for advancing women's careers. Now I want to work in Washington, but I'm confused and disappointed. There are very few female role models here, and with few exceptions, people with names

like John and Harry and Joe still run the place. Is this a good town for a woman to work and succeed?

A: I am going to push back gently on your characterization of Washington as an estrogen-free zone. While there may not be as many women in senior roles as you and I would like, there are many, and there are plenty of women in very important jobs. Hillary Clinton was Obama's Secretary of State, and I think she'll go down in history as one of the best in that job. Three women sit on the Supreme Court. The Chief of Police in Washington is a woman. Another had the top policy job at the Pentagon until recently, Bobbie Kilberg heads up one of the most influential technology groups in the country, the Northern Virginia Technology Council, and she's a mom with five kids. Marne Levine was chief of staff at the National Economic Council, and then somebody at Facebook was smart enough to hire her to head up their global public policy. There are 81 women in the House of Representatives and 20 in the Senate.

I must confess, however, that I'm a "glass is half-full" girl, so I bounced your question off NBC correspondent Andrea Mitchell, one of the best and most respected journalists—male or female—in the country. She is Chief Foreign Affairs Correspondent for NBC and hosts her own show on MSNBC, and has covered energy, the White House, State, campaigns and international crises. She has worked in Washington since 1976. She says she's seen progress for women in D.C., although it has come slowly.

"Washington moves at a snail's pace when it comes to advancement for women in politics," Andrea says. "In politics, we certainly have powerful women in key places, and since Madeline Albright, we have become accustomed to a woman Secretary of State. But until recently, the Senate and the White House have mostly been an all-boys club. More women are playing major roles in lobbying, law, and public relations. There is now a woman at the top of NBC and several women in major Executive Producer roles in the media. The late Katharine Graham was long the only woman on prestigious media boards. Washington is still not an easy place for women to work, but it is becoming more possible to break through."

I am even more positive: I think this is a good town for women to work and succeed in, in part because it tends to be a busy place where people are just trying to get the job done. The person—male or female—who works hard and focuses on his/her organization's goals is going to be embraced. And before people start yelling at me, yes, I know there are exceptions (see the clown above). And yes, I know there are guys who feel threatened by women in the workplace.

So you're not in the office fantasy baseball league? Don't worry about that. Do worry, though, if you're not in key meetings or given enough access to the principal to do your job properly. Do you have the resources you need to get your job done? If not, those are issues you need to address.

Let's say you stick around—and I hope you do—and work your way up to a senior role. You will have many challenges, but few will be because you wear a skirt. Emily Bazelon had a terrific interview with Supreme Court Justice Ruth Bader Ginsburg in the *New York Times* that was largely about women and the Supreme Court. Ginsburg, who was one of only nine women in a law school class of 500 in the late '50s, doesn't dwell much on being female in a male-dominated role. "If you're going to change things," she told Bazelon, "you have to be with the people who hold the levers."

I love that. Don't worry so much about John and Harry and Joe. Focus on your work and know that there are lots of Andreas and Nancys and Hillarys in this town, too.

Q: Does a woman have to behave differently when working with a bunch of guys?

A: "Be yourself" is a trite but good rule of life in most situations... within reason. Keep the chitchat about your book club to a minimum, because few of your male colleagues share your enthusiasm for *50 Shades of Grey*. Similarly, don't expect them to behave differently just because you're around.

One of the best things that happened to me at the Pentagon was meeting Army Colonel George Rhynedance and Major Riccoh Player, my military assistants. Both of them are exceptional people, and both of them are very male. Their guidance contributed greatly to any successes I had there. Work your way through the mind-numbing maze of military bureaucracy? They knew how. Develop a crisis management plan for a large and diverse department? They'd knock that out in their sleep. Wrangle the Pentagon press corps, a notoriously independent gang? No problem. I like to think they respected me as a colleague and boss. I know they didn't look at me as a woman first. And occasionally that could be a problem.

On most mornings I headed to work well before the sun or my kids were up. Trying not to disturb my sleeping family, I would shower and dress quickly, often in the dark. In the dark you don't really see the buttons on your lovely yellow Valentino suit. And once I got to the Pentagon, I am running. Maybe thirty minutes in my office to read a few briefings Rhynedance had ready for me, then a quick conversation with Riccoh about an upcoming trip. A reporter sticks his head in for a quick status check on some issue. Even before I head upstairs for my first real meeting of the day—at 6:30 am— Rhynedance, Riccoh and I have seen each other several times.

After that meeting, I stop by the front office to see if the travel agenda for the next trip is done, chat with a few people in the hallway and head back to my office, interrupted along the way by a handful of roving reporters. Before I know it, it's almost 9, and I make a quick stop at the large and brightly lit ladies room near my office. And then I see them. The buttons on my lovely yellow Valentino suit have been carefully wrapped in aluminum foil by the dry cleaner. It's something nice dry cleaners do and something few Army Colonels and Marine Majors know about.

I ripped the foil off the buttons and headed into my office. I always thought Rhynedance and Riccoh had a GPS device planted on me because they were always standing and waiting for me when I came into the office, no matter how quietly I approached. And there they were, looking impressive in their spiffy uniforms.

"What the heck were you thinking?" I asked them, a small part of me suspecting this was a joke they had played on me.

"What do you mean, ma'am? Rhynedance said.

"The aluminum foil on my buttons? It didn't occur to either of you to say something?"

Rhynedance and Riccoh shared a look and tried not to laugh.

"I'm so sorry, ma'am," Rhynedance—the senior officer accepting responsibility—said. "We thought it was some fashion thing."

So yes, don't be afraid to work in an all-male environment if it's a job you are passionate about. Just don't count on your colleagues for help with the girl stuff.

Q: As one of the few female Chiefs of Staff on the Hill, I'm frequently profiled in those *Women to Watch*-type pieces. It helps my boss to have a woman running his shop, but such coverage can breed resentment in the staff, and the publications are often geared toward women. I'm worried about not being taken seriously if I show up in *Vogue*. Should I do them or stay in the shadows?

A: *Politico* and *Huffington Post*? Sure. *Elle* and *Vogue*? Maybe, if they've hired a veteran, respected journalist to do a piece on women on Capitol Hill. Does the reporter have a solid body of work? Are they fair or do they take cheap shots? And in those interviews repeatedly highlight your boss's accomplishments, not yours; the entire staff's efforts, not just your hard work. Be maddeningly gracious. And be very careful about photos, because they can make a lasting impression that is difficult to erase.

Few people could say no to Karen Hughes, President George W. Bush's communications guru, so when she called me at the Pentagon to say that Rumsfeld would be joining the President and other members of the "war cabinet" for an Annie Leibovitz photo-shoot for *Vanity Fair*, I winced. I knew Rumsfeld would hate the idea. Heck, I hated it. We were just a few weeks past the 9/11 attacks and, to put it mildly, we were a little busy. Not to mention the inevitable questions about the propriety of the Secretaries of State and Defense, the head of the CIA, the National Security Advisor, and the President making time for something as frivolous as a pretty picture for a magazine obsessed with movie stars.

I was wrong. Telling Rumsfeld turned out not to be the worst part of this ordeal. I doubt he knew anything about Leibovitz, a renowned photographer, but he faked it well. (As we got closer to the shoot date, he kept asking about "your friend, Amy the photographer.") The worst part turned out to be that someone (many now deny their role) decided it would be a good idea to shoot several of the communication types involved in the war effort as well. The stated rationale for this photo was that communications played a huge role in the war on terror, so those in charge of communications should be included. White House Press Secretary Ari Fleischer would be in it. So would White

House Communications Director Dan Bartlett and Mary Matalin and Charlotte Beers, briefly the head of Public Diplomacy and Public Affairs at the State Department. (Karen was smart enough to keep herself out of it.) As a failed photographer, I knew enough to realize that the shoot was not going to be our finest moment. Little did I realize how bad it would be. Once we got our principals (Rumsfeld, Dick Cheney, Condoleezza Rice...) through their shoot in the White House, we all raced next door to a porch off the Old Executive Office Building. It was a grayish day, and Amy/Annie had an army of assistants fussing with cameras and lights. She brought her own makeup person, too, but spray paint wouldn't have covered the bags under our eyes or the creases on our foreheads. Amy/Annie gave each of us about two minutes of repair work with her makeup maven.

Initially, Leibovitz had all of us—guys and gals—piled together, but she soon moved Ari and Dan closer to the porch's opening, where some softer light was coming in, while Mary and I were pushed farther into the shadows. Part of me hoped this might be good (we'd be out of sight?), but my fading photography skills warned me it wasn't. But never mind. We were in a rush to get back to work, so we thanked Amy/Annie and her team and raced back to our jobs. "Boy, that sucked," I told Rhynedance over the phone as I headed back across the river.

Weeks go by. During that time, Brian had to pick up a lot of the slack at home. Actually, he had to do everything—birthdays, doctors' appointments, play dates and all the care and feeding of our kids. So on the occasional Sunday evening that I was home, I would leave Brian with a bottle of wine and take the kids out for some quality time—burgers and fries at a sports bar, followed by a quick wander through Barnes and Noble.

So there we were in a bookstore on a Sunday in early December. "Hey," I said to my kids, "let's check out the magazines." I'd heard our issue of *Vanity Fair* was out, and I was warily interested to see how our shoot turned out. As we approached the magazine rack, I thought, "Hmmm... That's not something you see around here every day." Gathered in front of the magazine rack were several 20-somethings, looking very Goth in black, chains and multiple piercings. They looked very out of place in Bethesda, land of Dockers and loafers.

Colin saw the cover first. "It's your boss, Mom! It's your boss!" Even though they had no idea what he was talking about, Devan and Charlie chimed in, causing a few heads to turn our way. There in the hands of the head Goth was the "War Team" issue of *Vanity Fair*. The head Goth quickly flipped through the magazine and stopped at the center foldout. Propelled forward by my eager if clueless kids, we were just feet away when he got to our picture.

Colin peeked over the Goth's shoulder and screamed, "Mommy, it's you, it's you!" Everyone within shouting distance was looking at us now, and I was looking for a rock to crawl under. Oblivious to the excitement around him, head Goth laughed loudly and said, "Wow, look at those bitches. Talk about rode hard and put up wet!"

Somehow I knew he wasn't talking about Ari and Dan.

WHEN YOU WORRY ABOUT BEING TAKEN
SERIOUSLY, IT'S ALREADY TOO LATE.

CHAPTER FOUR

MAKING DECISIONS AND STICKING TO THEM...
OR NOT

"Captain Queeg and His Diet Cokes"

Q: I spent the last 10 months working hard to get a plum job at a non-profit in town. In addition to doing several lengthy interviews with senior staff, I had former colleagues and bosses call, write and email on my behalf. The good news: they hired me. The sort of bad news: I was just offered an even better job in the Administration. It's a once-in-a-lifetime opportunity I'd love to grab, but I worry about burning bridges with all the people who went to bat for me.

A: That's a good concern, but most people in D.C. understand goals and dreams, and we all know that timing can be a cruel thing. Just when you head down one avenue, another one opens up. As I said earlier, my career has included many careers, which required me to sometimes jump quickly.

After six years working for John McCain, I thought it was time to work in the private sector. I accepted a wonderful job with Jim Lake, one of the best communications hands in town. Before the ink was dry on my new business cards I leapt at the chance to work for Carla A. Hills, the U.S. Trade Representative (USTR). Jim wished me well and even gave me some good advice. A few years later I moved into my new gig at Edelman Public Relations only to hop across town five months later to work at the National Cable Television Association (NCTA). There was no "I'm doing this for my country!" excuse that time—the NCTA job was just flat-out better. The folks at Edelman were gracious and supportive as I waved goodbye.

Since I've been guilty of jumping early and often, I am recusing myself and pulling in Wendy Pangburn, a veteran Washington headhunter with a stellar reputation for placing senior executives at leading trade associations, non-profits and major corporations. She's seen the best and worst of behavior and knows what can influence a person's long-term reputation.

"Fact: she did reach out to others for assistance," Wendy says. "Fact: she accepted and made a commitment *and* started the job. Fact: she will burn bridges if she bails.

"Life isn't always fair. Be happy with a new job that will still be around after this Administration is gone."

Wendy makes a good case. Clearly you have skills appreciated by many, and there will be more Administration opportunities down the road.

Q: As head of Congressional Liaison for a federal agency, I encourage frequent contact with Capitol Hill, and I try hard to maintain a good working relationship with members and their staff, even if we often disagree on issues. Many in our building—including the Cabinet officer and several senior staffers—disagree. They say we should tell Congress as little as possible. As luck would have it, the last time the Secretary

had a "private" conversation with a House member it was leaked before we got back to our building. I wake up at 4 a.m. sweating bullets over this. Who's right?

A: You are. On even the best days, members of Congress can drive you crazy, but they have jobs to do and you have an obligation to keep them informed. Yes, they leak and bloviate and often infuriate, but somebody voted for them.

Remind your colleagues that it's always better to play offense than defense. Schedule visits to Hill offices, briefings for Members and their staffs and trips to your agency as often as possible. And make sure you are bipartisan in your outreach. Many of those meetings will be sparsely attended, but it's important that you make the effort.

And please stop waking up at 4 a.m. about this. You're doing the right thing. I had a few of those very early wakeup calls myself as we spent months developing the embedding program that sent hundreds of journalists into combat at the start of the Iraq war. The goal was simple: encourage as much coverage as possible of the war—the good, the bad and the ugly. As word of the potential program got out in late 2002, concerns grew for many serious people. Early on, I had doubts myself. Some said the American people couldn't handle the images they might see during the first-ever live coverage of combat. I disagreed completely. I knew the American people could handle the truth. Others said reporters couldn't be trusted to not reveal information that could put an operation at risk. That was a definite possibility, I thought, since many embeds would not be familiar with national security issues. Still others said the military, already burdened by unconventional warfare this time, could not handle the extra burden of media crawling all over them. That, too, was a legitimate worry. Were the benefits of transparency worth the extra load we'd be putting on the military's back? I argued that they would.

Not everyone agreed, though, even after weeks of consultation throughout the Administration. Several senior officials voiced their objections to Dan Bartlett, head of White House Communications and one of President Bush's closest advisors. Dan worked hard to listen to the communication heads at all agencies. Every few weeks he gathered senior communications staffers from throughout the Administration—even those not in national security—to brief them on pending war efforts. Occasionally he would have the President stop by to thank the assembled flacks.

At one of these sessions Dan asked me to brief the gang on the embedding program. There were lots of issues raised. White House Press Secretary Ari Fleischer worried that people might see their loved ones killed or injured on live TV. I understood his point but argued the benefits of a bright spotlight on military action outweighed the downside. Ari and I argued our cases for a few minutes.

In the midst of this, the President strolls in, so Dan asked me to give a quick overview of the embed program to the President. As I briefed President Bush, I could tell he was listening closely. When I was done, he stood up and said, "Well, it sounds crazy, but I guess you know what you're doing." With a laugh he good-naturedly punched me in the shoulder and walked out.

As you might have guessed by now, we did the embed program, and it was everything I had hoped it would be.

You know you're right on this issue. Seek out opportunities to meet with the members of Congress and their staffs, especially when it's not about the crisis du jour. Keep them in the loop on the seemingly mundane yet important news about your agency. Slowly but surely build up support for what you and your colleagues do on behalf of the taxpayers, their constituents. Build strong relationships because you know there will be fights down the road. If you can't convince your Secretary and colleagues to go along with your approach, you may have to part ways. Shutting out Congress, no matter how annoying they may be, is no way to keep a good reputation in this town.

Q: How long do I have to be in a job before I can quit? I signed up with a prominent lobbying firm without doing much due diligence. I was seduced by a good salary and lots of perks, but I didn't know the head of the office rivaled Captain Queeg in paranoia, only his obsession is Diet Coke rather than strawberries. I didn't know most of the senior partners are sloths who spend many hours at the Palm each week reminiscing about the good old days (the'80s and '90s!). Most important, I didn't realize our work consists mainly of making sure campaign checks get to the right members of Congress. I screwed up. I know it. But I'm miserable! I don't know if I even want to be a lobbyist anymore. Can I split after just a few weeks or do I have to tough it out?

A: It's almost never okay to quit after a few weeks, and I'll bet the senior executives in your firm do more than count Diet Cokes and chug martinis at the Palm. If they are giving you a good salary and perks they must be making some clients happy. And while much lobbying work these days is transactional (who sends a check to whom?), there is still much work done to help assess the political landscape, draft legislation or build coalitions to prevent onerous regulations. There is value to lobbying, and I bet you'll find some in your firm if you look around.

Your situation falls under what I call the "Devil Wears Prada" rule. You made a bad decision, and you have to ride it out. Remind yourself that a million gals would kill for your job and be happy that you have gainful employment. Even if you're miserable, fake a good attitude and stick it out for at least a year. Anything less, and your resume will raise questions you don't want to answer.

Even savvy professionals at very high levels make impulsive career moves they come to regret. (Yes, I'm talking about me!) When Bob Dole ran for President in 1996 he smartly hired John Buckley as his communications director. John, the veteran of several national campaigns, was so persuasive that he convinced me, then six months pregnant, to join the campaign to help launch Dole's running mate in August. I happened to bump into Roderick DeArment, the head of the Dole Vice Presidential search process, and I asked him how the search was going. With a groan he said, "I think I'm one of the few people in politics who hasn't cheated on his wife or forgotten to pay his taxes."

One of those few decent V.P. contenders was Jack Kemp, former New York Congressman and former star quarterback for the Buffalo Bills. Kemp, who died in 2009, had a huge personality and enough energy to power a Honda hybrid. That energy, coupled with charm and smart, forward-looking economic policies, made him a good complement to Dole's more "mature" persona, to put it nicely.

As several of us descended on Dole's birthplace of Russell, Kansas, to prepare for the announcement event, word of Kemp's selection leaked out. We didn't mind because it generated some buzz and excitement, two things rarely seen in the Dole campaign. As John headed to the airport to collect Kemp and bring him back to Russell to meet with Dole, we scouted the site (hay bales in a square or in rows?), prepared Dole's remarks (Will he even look at them?), and wagered on how much of a bump the Kemp announcement would give us (At least five points, right?).

A few minutes before Jack and John were scheduled to arrive I got a phone call. "We have a problem," John said.

"We're all good here," I chirped, missing the urgent tone of his voice. "What's up?"

"He doesn't want to do it," John said, and now it sounded like he was covering the phone's mouthpiece as he spoke.

"Who doesn't want to do *what*?"

"Kemp does not want to run. I got him in the car, but I don't know if I can get him there."

"You have got to be kidding me," I said. "He can't do that. Everyone knows he's Dole's nominee. He told Dole he would do it. He *has* to do it!"

As I said, John's a very persuasive guy, and he somehow convinced Kemp to do it. And Kemp went on to be a terrific running mate for Dole. I was fortunate to spend about four weeks with him and quickly became a fan. Despite his initial misgivings—like you, Kemp probably did not think through his career move when he agreed to run—he worked hard, stayed cheerful through the toughest days and kept spirits up when the drag of the campaign got staffers down.

There was probably more potential upside for Kemp than for you at the lobbying firm, but there's a relevant theme for both experiences: Tough it out, do the best you can, and you might be surprised at what you'll discover. At worst, you will learn how to work under tough conditions, always a handy skill to have.

Q: How do you know you've stayed somewhere too long? I have lobbied at the same trade association for eight years, moving up from assistant level to vice president. I like the issues (entertainment) and the people (colorful) but worry that if I stay too long I'll have a hard time

transitioning to another job. I also think it would be good to live and work outside Washington for a while.

A: First, it *would* be very good for you to live outside Washington for a while. Second, when you leave this job depends a lot on where you want to go. One of the great things about a trade association job is that your members get to know you and vice versa. It's almost like an internship, only with much better pay and benefits. Do you and your significant other have and/or want kids? If so, move when they're young. They'll complain less than teenagers will.

If you want to transition to the operations side of a company, go now before you've "golden-handcuffed" yourself to your current position.

Often, it's not obvious when it's time to go. I wrestled with when to leave John McCain's office, weighing the pros (he was a blast to work for) and cons (six years is a long time to be a Hill press secretary). My indecision ended when John and others pointed out I was enjoying the Keating Five scandal way too much. Most of the people in McCain's orbit were distraught and even panicked by the all-consuming and ferocious media coverage, but I was loving the challenge it presented. That was a very clear sign that it was time to do something new.

Sometimes the signs are more obvious. Hardly a week goes by that I don't think wistfully about my Pentagon job. Important issues, phenomenal team and the life of a 1960s suburban dad—what could be better? That's what I thought, selfishly, at the time. Brian and I had several relatives, including his dad, my sister and mother, and our daughter all facing serious health issues. I thought I was being helpful and supportive to all, but I had no idea how much it all added to Brian's "Mr. Mom" workload.

Coming home one Thursday night, not too late (I thought), I overheard Brian talking to my dad on the phone. "Charlie, I could be up there tomorrow but have to be back on Saturday because we have two soccer games and a birthday party," he said.

I don't know what help my dad needed, but I felt like I had been hit in the head with a hammer. I had been so selfish, piling all the normal home front duties on Brian's shoulders and then leaving him to help care for sick relatives at the same time.

"I have been so selfish," I thought, and knew then that I had to leave the best job I ever had. While I miss the Pentagon and the people there, I have no regrets about my decision.

You'll know when it's time to go.

THESE ARE YOUR CORE PRINCIPLES TODAY.

CHAPTER FIVE

HOW TO RECOVER FROM A MISTAKE

"Grovel Early, and Often"

Q: In a moment of anger, I swore at a staffer from my opponent's campaign. He was heckling me during my remarks and dressed as a chicken! Do I have to apologize?

A: Cluck yes! And quickly. If you don't believe me, just ask former Virginia Governor George Allen, who became the first political road-kill of the information revolution when he failed to recognize the volume and velocity of a bad story rocket-fueled by the Internet.

In 2006, Allen was in a close race against war hero Jim Webb, but as a former governor and son of legendary Washington Redskins coach George Allen, he was expected to win and then be a strong contender for the Republican presidential nomination in 2008. That is until a young Webb staffer who happened to be Indian-American showed up at an Allen event with a video camera. Ticked off at the staffer's mere presence (he wasn't a heckling chicken), Allen called him a "macaca." Few people at the event knew what Allen meant, but the Webb staffer knew he had drawn blood. Some say it is a common French racial slur; others say it comes from the French word "macaque"—monkey. Whatever it means, it was clear from the quickly viral video that Allen was not complimenting the young staffer.

Allen's first mistake was to insult the staffer. His second was to not apologize immediately. And his third mistake was to ignore the first mistake. Allen tried floating on denial for several days before he apologized. By that time hundreds of thousands of people and scores of media had made sure everyone knew he had used a racial slur. Most political observers say the gaffe—and, just as damning, how he handled it—sunk Allen in the senate race.

One of my mantras is "grovel early and often." In today's hyper-fast information environment, you have to make apologies even faster, admit mistakes more quickly and hope you've diverted the tsunami that could sink you.

Q: Uh, oops? I thought I was sending a personal tweet to my staff to vent about the knuckleheads across the aisle. It went public—insanely so. Calling a fellow member of the state's Congressional delegation a "pompous pinhead" may not have been smart, but he should recognize that it was a private communication, right?

A: Wrong. Nothing is private these days, especially if you are in public office. The good news is that technology allows you to reach thousands of people with a simple keystroke. The bad news is it's too easy to hit SEND without thinking. Just ask former Congressman and NYC Mayoral wannabee Anthony Weiner, who sexted himself into the private sector.

For starters, apologize. Immediately. In person, if possible. If not, call him—don't email or text him! And don't try that "I'm sorry if I offended you" drivel. That's the worst apology in the book, deployed by too many in the public eye. *Of course* you insulted him! I once told a reporter that Pat Buchanan, conservative commentator and GOP primary opponent to President George Herbert Walker Bush, would have to "crawl across broken glass on his hands and knees with his tongue hanging out" before we'd let him speak at the Republican convention. I thought I was off the record. Not. And not that it mattered—it was a stupid thing to say under any circumstances, and I instantly apologized to Buchanan, to the President and to Republicans in general. I apologized for days and thought about how to make sure I never again said something so stupid.

You should think about how you use communication devices. When in doubt, imagine how that Tweet would look on a billboard. Would you still hit SEND?

Q: Can something be truly off-the-record? I had drinks with a reporter recently, "just to catch up" as he put it. We chatted about our families, jobs and upcoming battles on the Hill. Six hours later I read—in horror—several of my comments in something he filed online. This was not an interview; it was a social event. I say he had no right to repeat our conversation. Our press secretary says I was an idiot to trust him.

A: Most people believe nothing is off-the-record, that if you say it or type it, it may show up somewhere. I disagree. There are reporters you can trust, but not many. They tend to be the smart ones with whom you have a long-standing relationship. They don't want to burn sources. Also, I'm betting you didn't say, "This whole conversation is off-the-record" as you ordered your first drink. In this town it's not an insult, it's just smart.

It's probably not much consolation, but many people have found themselves in the same situation, and with far greater consequences. John McCain is one of the best when it comes to dealing with the media. Because of all the time he spends with the working press he feels very comfortable around them. Sometimes, too loose. When first elected to Congress, McCain's fresh take on issues and self-deprecating humor made him popular with many reporters. Veteran journalists like David Broder and George Will touted him as a rising young star of the Republican Party.

Early in the summer of 1988, R.W. "Johnny" Apple of the *New York Times* called me to say he wanted to stop by the office "just to catch up." He and McCain had known each other for years, going back to when McCain served in Vietnam and Apple was covering the war for the *Times*. Being a dutiful press secretary, normally I sat in on all of McCain's interviews. Most of the time, my role was to be an attentive potted plant, because McCain didn't need any help answering questions or driving home his talking points. He and Apple assured me they weren't going to talk about anything important, so, respecting their friendship, I headed into my office next door.

For over an hour I heard laughter and a lot of table-slapping, and more laughter. I couldn't tell what they were talking about, but it didn't sound like anything serious. When Apple walked out of McCain's office, I said, "You guys didn't get into any trouble in there, did you?" They both laughed and said, "Of course not."

But of course they did. The next day, the following quote ran on the front page of the *New York Times*: *"He's all fuzzed up. Nobody knows who he is or what he stands for," said freshman Arizona Senator John McCain.*

The "he" was then Vice President Bush, and Apple's story was about Bush's struggles to move beyond President Reagan's shadow as he ran for President in 1988.

"Oh my God" was all I could blurt out when I got a call early that morning from the first of the many reporters amazed that John would say something like that to the *New York Times*, and, by the way, "Will he say it to me, too?"

"Oh my God" is all John could say when I called him at home a few minutes later to let him know that his knucklehead "off-the-record" comments to his best pal Johnny Apple were the news headline of the day. To his credit, he didn't blame Apple; he blamed himself. And the first thing he did was call Vice President Bush to apologize. "It was stupid, and I shouldn't have said it," McCain told Bush. Bush accepted the apology graciously and told John not to worry.

John learned a lesson that day, and I sat in on every interview he did after that. Sadly, your press secretary is right; you were stupid to trust the reporter. It doesn't mean you can't or won't trust one again, but always make the ground rules clear. And just because you value personal allegiances, don't assume that reporters do. They value a good story over a good friendship almost every time.

Q: I communicate constantly with staff, colleagues, friends, family and supporters by email and text. Recently I mistakenly forwarded an email to my legislative director. I thought I had sent him some smart thoughts on energy legislation. Instead, I sent him a long email trail in which my chief of staff and I questioned the staffer's abilities and commitment to the job. Other than apologizing profusely—which I have done—what can I do?

A: Uh, have you started looking for a new legislative director? If I were he, I'd quit.

As you now know, if you say it or write it—on any device—it can get out. There's no such thing as privacy in the digital world. Conversations about staffers' work habits are probably best handled in a face-to-face conversation, by the way, even the positive ones. I had a near-death experience with some digital eavesdropping during the '92 presidential campaign that has always made me think of my mobile phone as a ticking time-bomb.

Among the many mistakes of the ill-fated Bush-Quayle '92 campaign was President Bush's order that no one was to comment on candidate Bill Clinton's personal life. Although many people—heck, even some of his best friends—called him a draft-dodging, philandering, pot smoker, none of us did. We got no gold stars for good behavior, though, and got slammed for simply repeating what one of Clinton's staffers said about him.

On almost every campaign—win or lose—there are ups and downs, good weeks and bad weeks. But not on that Bush-Quayle campaign. We started sliding in February of '92 and never looked up again. Bob Teeter, God rest his soul, was one of our three campaign managers, pollster and eternal optimist.

"This is just like the Gerald Ford campaign," he'd say, pounding on his desk, trying to boost our spirit. "We hit rock-bottom, and once we got passed Labor Day it was all uphill." We were all too polite to remind him that Ford lost that race.

As the days dragged, our expectations lowered. A good week? Heck, we'd take a good hour. And we finally thought we had one.

President Bush was headed to South Carolina for a campaign event. We had the umpteenth version of our economic vision to unveil and felt that maybe, just maybe we could get on offense.

Not. Bright and early my phone rings because Mary Matalin was accused, wrongly, of associating Candidate Clinton with bimbos. What she had done was quote Clinton aide Betsy Wright, who coined the term "bimbo eruptions" to describe the swirling rumors of Clinton affairs. It didn't matter. In the bizarre world of presidential politics, many in the media declared that Mary had violated our oft-stated principle to not go negative.

It was bad. Mary called me at about 5:30 a.m. "Well, this stinks," she said. We agreed that it would be best if she stayed home that day.

"I can beat them back," I said cheerfully—and stupidly. We were going to lay out some bright and shiny talking points on the economy, for gosh sakes!

This "scandal" was like crack cocaine to our press corps. Even in that pre-Internet era, news traveled quickly, and the media frenzy was underway before 9:00 a.m.

For the first hour or so I stoically ignored the yammering of the press corps. Soon, though, it was obvious that "our team" was not going along with my game plan. "You know folks at the White House are really ticked about this?" said one reporter traveling with us.

"I'm sure you're overstating that," I swatted back, while thinking, "Which SOB is talking to reporters about this?"

"Will Mary apologize to Governor Clinton?" asked another who was getting drowned out by the Jack Russell terrier lookalike who kept yapping, "Why did she say it? Why did she say it?"

"I don't think an apology is necessary," I said, pointedly turning my back to the terrier and wondering if a quick apology might staunch the bleeding. More annoying than the press corps were the White House and campaign staffers bleating at me throughout the morning. "This is not good," sniffed one. "What are you guys going to do about it?" As if we weren't on the same team!

Every hour or so, I would check in with Mary on my cell phone, which was about the size of a shoebox back then. "I think it might be okay," I lied to her. "The reporters are asking the same things over and over. I get that, but I'm ticked that some of our people are feeding their frenzy."

Mary was devastated that she'd hurt the President, and ticked at our wimpy colleagues. It was one thing not to fight back—tactically it might have made sense. But go on background to criticize her? That, as she put it bluntly, "really sucked." And it got worse.

As the morning grinded on, I kept insisting that Mary hadn't connected Clinton to bimbos—his own advisor had done that. "Talk to the Clinton-Gore campaign," I'd say in a falsely optimistic tone. "They're the ones you should be talking to about this." Fat chance.

As others ate box lunches, I slipped away to confer with Mary. This time there was no false hope. "This is awful," I whimpered. "And the worst part is that our own people are going south on us!"

Mary and I talked several times that day. Every conversation involved us swapping news and profanities about the colleagues betraying us. And by now, it was "us"—*Thelma and Louise*, as we were once dubbed in the press—against the world.

"Come on, Torie," the Jack Russell kept yapping, tugging on my sleeve as I walked past him. "Why did she say it?"

We were scheduled to be wheels up mid-afternoon to head back to Andrews Air Force base and Washington. Foolishly thinking I could turn the day's focus to the President's awesome economic speech, I headed back into the warehouse that was serving as the filing center for the traveling press corps. They were all typing furiously, barking into cell phones and showing more energy than they had for months. The atmosphere was electric—and made me think of an electric chair.

They swarmed me, pushing and shoving, barking and growling, shouting questions. In the middle of the pack, jumping up and down to be seen in the throng, the Jack Russell yelled yet again, "Come on, Torie, why did she say it? Why did she say it?"

That was it. I broke, and yelled, "Because it's the truth, damn it!"

Suddenly, keyboards stopped clicking and jaws started dropping. I had just made a bad story worse.

Furious—and fully aware of what I had done—I headed out to the motorcade that would take us to the plane. I crawled into my seat and refused to talk with anyone other than the steward who offered me a glass of wine.

When we landed at Andrew's, I went straight to my car for the drive back to the campaign headquarters. I checked in with Lori Muir, my amazing assistant.

"You've got a lot of messages," she said as I heard her riffling through her pile of pink phone messages. She ticked off calls from every major print and electronic outlet in the world. "Uh oh," she said, stopping on what would have been about the 12th phone message.

"What?" I said, thinking nothing could make the day worse.

"Well," she said slowly, knowing I was about to have my head explode, "a reporter with the Charleston paper somehow overheard several of your cell phone conversations with Mary—maybe over a police scanner? He wants to talk with you about them."

I shouted "Oh my God!" as I jerked my car to the shoulder of the Suitland Parkway. "You have got to be kidding me!"

Most people would think I was worried about what my bosses would think if our conversations became public. Remember, we had trashed everybody we could think of that day—the campaign managers, our colleagues, Vice President, the President and probably the President's dog. We were furious and swearing like sailors in a profanity contest.

But that wasn't my main concern at that moment. What made my hands shake and my stomach churn was the thought of my parents reading the kind of language we had used. They would have been appalled. I told Lori I would call her back, jumped out of the car and threw up on the shoulder. This being rush hour, several happy commuters honked their approval as they drove by.

"Well," I thought. "I've never written a letter of resignation before. This will be educational."

I know people love to hate lawyers, but I love at least one. Bobby Burchfield was the campaign's General Counsel. When I could get back in my car and had mostly stopped shaking, I got him on the phone and explained what had happened, leaving out the part about losing my lunch. He calmly took charge of the situation: he got the reporter's bosses and his newspaper's legal counsel on the phone and reminded them of the laws governing overhearing—and then printing—private phone conversations. The paper then buried what was probably the biggest scoop of that reporter's life.

Ever since that day, I've had a huge fear of cell phones, and I try hard not to have any sensitive conversations on cell phones or via emails or texts. Day-to-day stuff, like scheduling meetings—no problem. Catching up with a friend after the weekend—fine. But have the important chats on landlines or in face-to-face conversations. And if you just can't help yourself, and you have to tweet and blog and text, then accept the risks that go along with that behavior and get ready to someday be standing by the side of the road, puking.

Q: We work for a two-term member of Congress facing a tough primary opponent with a formidable research team. They've accused our boss of "complete fabrications" in his resume and are calling on us to put the record straight. It's true he once listed UCLA as his alma mater, even though he only studied there for a year, and it's also true that the "successful real estate practice" he claimed to have had was an internship in his mother's firm when he was in his 20s. Other than that, his resume is accurate and up to date. Should we ignore the attacks?

A: In the good old days (when there were printed newspapers people read, a few broadcast news outlets and some well-known and respected rules of the game), you could play the "Don't engage them" card. The volume and velocity with which information travels now makes that approach obsolete. Fair or not, the general rule now is "Charges unanswered are charges accepted as fact," and if you don't respond, many voters will believe the accusations.

Your boss starts in a credibility hole, thanks to the creative writing on his resume. You don't need to go door-to-door to do *mea culpas* at every home in your district, but you do need to clear up his record.

YOU JUST WENT VIRAL ASSAULTING
POULTRY. THERE IS NO "BOUNCE."

CHAPTER SIX

MANAGING UP WITHOUT LETTING YOURSELF DOWN

"And That's Why I Turned to Theft..."

Q: Several of us think our boss is having an affair with his executive assistant. At first, we thought they just had a very good working relationship. Then we noticed that they always show up and leave work at the same time. And now she travels with him, although the office manager says the boss pays for two rooms. He's just a Congressman and not even in the leadership. Does he really need her help attending fundraisers at the races in Saratoga in August? He's married, by the way, with a lovely wife and kids back home. Maybe it's none of our business, but if we've noticed it so have others on the Hill, which means it's only a matter of time before a reporter asks us about their 'special relationship.' Maybe we're wrong about them, but we feel like they're jeopardizing his career, and ours. Should we draw straws to see who has to ask him about it?

A: As my friend the garden guru says, "If it looks like something has been chewing on your plants, something has probably been chewing on your plants." I suspect you and your colleagues are right.

Don't worry—you can put the straws down: I don't think any

of you are the best person to talk with him about this, and besides, some Congressmen have been known to shoot the messenger. Then they hold tearful news conferences to say how truly sorry they are about hurting their family and loyal staff. (But I digress.)

Enlist one of your favorite campaign consultants to have that awkward conversation. Learn from Peter Scher, once a top aide to former U.S. Senator John Edwards, who confronted the North Carolina senator before his 2008 presidential primary campaign, over suspicions he was having an affair with the campaign "documentarian," Rielle Hunter. "I told him if it was true that he was having an affair with Ms. Hunter, he should not run for president," Scher testified at Edwards' campaign finance trial in 2012. "If it was true, eventually it would come out and it would destroy his political career."

Note that "if," and encourage your messenger to take the same approach. Unless you were in the room with them when they were canoodling, you don't know the nature of their relationship. But "if" he is having an affair, it *will* come out and ruin his political career and the lives of many around him. There is nowhere for that kind of information to hide these days.

Like Edwards, your boss may deny the affair and tell the confronter to "go ***k himself" as Edwards did to Scher. But you tried and then you have a choice: stay with him until the story breaks, or, as Scher did, get that resume dusted off and devote your energy to a candidate or a cause you can actually believe in.

Q: I work for a Cabinet Secretary who is smart, experienced and works harder than everybody else in the office. Her husband travels for his work, their kids are grown, and there's no family dog. In other words, she's free to work 24/7—and does. And none of us can keep up. Every night ends with her "Here are a few things to discuss tomorrow... " texts, and every day starts bright and early with "Please see me about

the attached… " emails in our inboxes. She's a digital machine! We're so busy reacting to her incoming that we can't get other work done. Much of what she focuses on is important, but this is insane. Other than pledging to never again work for someone without small, distracting children at home, how do we survive this madness?

A: I feel your pain. Working for people who have children is the best. I pledged to only work for people with *several* small children after my stint with U.S. Trade Representative Carla Hills, the hardest-working woman in Washington. None of us could keep up. Years later, I broke that pledge when I went to the Pentagon. People would ask me how I could ever work for Defense Secretary Rumsfeld, considered by many a demanding boss. "Easy," I'd say, "I worked for Carla Hills."

Almost everyone who makes it to a Cabinet position is hard-working and demanding. And if you can't handle the pressure you should step aside and clear a spot for the thousands of people who would eat their own children for a shot at your job. But just telling you to "man up" probably doesn't help much, so here are two ideas. First, appeal to your Chief of Staff, who is responsible for making the agency operate at maximum efficiency, which includes protecting the staff from a meltdown. Second, if your boss has a spouse or significant other, quietly appeal to that person. They probably would like to spend more time with their loved one and might conspire with you on ways to save some weekends and holidays.

As good as she was at handling her husband, Joyce Rumsfeld could not protect us from the dreaded snowflakes, the thousands of memos Rumsfeld sent out to staff, colleagues, families and friends. They ranged from the simple ("When will we brief the press again?") to the prophetic ("Aren't we going to need 21st century policies to deal with detainees in unconventional warfare?"). And as Thom Shanker once wrote in the *New York Times*, the sterner ones, "landed with anything but the silent gracefulness of their namesake."

Every snowflake came with the same mandate: *Attention must be paid*. And Rumsfeld had a ruthlessly effective way of making sure you responded to his snowflakes promptly. The system was a marvel in simplicity:

First, Rumsfeld dictates a snowflake into a little handheld recorder. Example:

> *To: Torie*
> *Re: Vanity Fair Photo Shoot*
> *Why is this on my schedule? Whose dumb idea was this?*
> *Please respond within 24 hours.*

Several times a day his assistants typed up the snowflakes. After being initialed by DR, they would float to my inbox as a copy went back to the SecDef.

On the massive desk in his office (it once belonged to Blackjack Pershing), Rumsfeld kept folders for each of the 10-15 staffers who, depending on their level of arrogance, considered themselves senior staffers key to the running of the Department. (I called them "village of the damned.") Every time a snowflake floated your way, a copy also went into your folder on Rumsfeld's desk. It didn't take long to realize this was DR's way to a) have people react to his outbox, not theirs; and b) spare his mind from being cluttered with tasks best delegated.

During the workday, you might head into DR's office a few minutes before a staff meeting to catch him alone on some issue enormously important to you. Maybe it was the idiot in Policy who kept trying to do briefings on Middle East affairs. Maybe it was your suggestion that he do an interview with David Letterman's mom at the Olympics. Whatever it was, it was important and it was your agenda, damn it.

With impeccable timing, DR would stop you in the middle of your first thoughtful sentence to say, "Let's look at your folder, shall we?" and flip through your snowflakes. He wanted to know what you had done/were doing/why haven't you done something? about the issues raised in the snowflakes.

Before you know it—and before you can stammer out an excuse, colleagues are filing in for the scheduled meeting, and you're toast. And there were dozens of snowflakes each week. Mondays were blizzard days, since Rumsfeld may have been alone Sunday afternoon with his little mini-recorder.

People coped in different ways. Many worked feverishly to always respond quickly and thoughtfully. Others tried and often failed to stay on top of their snowflakes. A very few—actually, just one—became conscientious objectors. Steve Cambone, a brainy guy with a laser-like focus on what's important, knew that reacting to every one of DR's snowflakes when they fell was not the best use of his time. Even more important, he had the confidence to know that he could (respectfully) refuse to engage in one of DR's impromptu folder perusals. Cambone was our hero, a Zeus of snowflake management.

I was no hero. I was a chicken. And that's why I turned to theft. When I knew there were problematic snowflakes in my folder, I would scoot into Rumsfeld's office when he was out. Pushing aside the bulging pile of snowflakes spilling out of my colleagues' folders, I'd quickly thumb through mine, and grab ones that had been keeping me up at night.

The next time I was near that infamous desk, I'd smile inwardly when the SecDef reached for my (suddenly slimmer!) folder.

Q: My boss is a two-term Senator from the Midwest, and a total stand-up guy. His first wife died, and he married our chief of staff from the state office. She's 20 years his junior and only worked for him for 18 months, but based on her behavior, you'd think she was the one the people elected. She sits in on staff meetings and offers opinions on everything. She calls the scheduler and adds things to her husband's calendar without asking anyone. She has way too many Chardonnay-fueled lunches with big donors and gets huffy if she's not publicly introduced at all her husband's events. Often the Senator comes to the office in the morning and says: "A good friend of mine was suggesting last night that we should (Your Ridiculous Idea Here)." We know the "good friend" is the spouse. Should we say something to him? To her? She can be brutal when crossed.

A: Pick a fight with your boss about his young, new wife? How do you think that will end? With you in the Senate Placement Office, seeking a new job? For starters, he's chosen her—twice. First as his chief of staff back home (so she must know something about your state) and then as his wife. So get over it, and do the Full Spousal Monty. Don't wait for her to speak up in staff meetings—ask for her opinion before lowly staffers speak. Seek her counsel on all issues, especially those affecting matters back home. Make her feel like the brilliant person she thinks she is. Let event organizers know your boss must really care about their group since he asked his wife to be there, so they'll want to introduce her in the never-ending game of sucking up played 24/7 in this town. And then make sure she's around when your outside legal counsel does the once-a-year ethics briefings, so she doesn't get you, her husband or herself in trouble with one of those Chardonnay-fueled lunches.

Q: I work for a three-term female member of Congress from the upper northwest. Her national name recognition is pretty good because party leadership frequently turns to her to present our case on social issues. It's easy to sort the interview requests she gets. Rachel Maddow—yes, Sean Hannity—no. But what to do with the request that she appear on *The Daily Show with Jon Stewart*? She wants to do it, but says, "Make sure we negotiate what we'll discuss." I'm pretty sure Stewart's folks don't negotiate with Hill staffers. Part of me—the part that wants to increase her national visibility and reputation—wants her to do it. The cautious side of me says this could be risky, and she'll kill me if she's embarrassed on his show.

A: Uh, oh. You work for one of those people who want fame without risks. My condolences. You're right, by the way—Stewart's staff will not negotiate with you. They'll barely speak to you in advance because they—unlike your boss—get the joke. It's not about your boss; it's about Jon Stewart. It's not about making her look good; it's about making him look smart and funny. And that's the way it should be.

I'm a longtime advocate of public officials seeking diverse vehicles to reach people, especially young people. Some of that advocacy was successful; some was not. I convinced former President George H.W. Bush to do an interview with Tabitha Soren, at the time MTV's wildly popular and very young political correspondent. We were shocked when she did not want to talk about Bush's plans to revive the economy or keep the country safe, but instead peppered him with repeated questions about the taxes on his family house in Kennebunkport, Maine. More successfully, I convinced many in the Pentagon, White House and State Department to engage with Al Jazeera, the Qatar-based Arab news channel that reaches tens of millions every day. Some in the Administration argued that Al Jazeera was biased and filled with spies. "You're probably right," I said, "but if we can reach Arab youth through them, that's a place I want to be."

And I argued that Administration officials should use late-night entertainment to reach people not glued to the major broadcast or cable news shows. "If 30 to 40 percent of young people get their news from late-night shows, then we should be on those shows!"

I soon found out that it's easy to tell others to appear on those shows, and it's a lot harder to do them myself. When I worked at the Pentagon, for reasons I still don't understand, Jon Stewart's people wanted me to appear on his show. Given my stern demeanor at the podium, maybe they thought they had the ultimate straight "man" for Stewart. Luckily for me, I had a great out: "She'd love to do the show," my favorite Air Force Colonel, Jay DeFrank, told Stewart's people. "But when the SecDef travels, she goes with him, and she just can't be away from the building when he's in town." That excuse happened to be true, and it worked for a long time.

One day Jay strolled into my office with a big smile. "Good news," he said, "Stewart's going to be in D.C. to tape, and they want you on." As the military likes to say, you lead from the front, and Jay appropriately—and with some glee—reminded me how often I had encouraged others to do late-night shows. Saying, "I'm probably going to regret this," I agreed and promptly forgot all about it as I tackled the real work of the day.

I also promptly forgot all the advice I give to those headed into interviews. *Know what you hope to accomplish in the interview. Think through the likely topics and questions. Practice.* I didn't prepare at all until I was driving across the 14th Street Bridge on a rainy Thursday night to tape with Stewart at a downtown studio. DeFrank and George Rhynedance, my Senior Military Assistant, had gone ahead of me.

Jay reached me on my cellphone as I was battling traffic. "Good news, I got a heads-up for you," he said. "The producers told us what Stewart wants to do on your segment—he loves military acronyms." I slowed down and ignored the cars honking at me. "I hate acronyms," I said. "I am the anti-military acronym queen. I've made a point of not learning acronyms." Now I'm fuming.

When I got to the studio, I faked a good attitude, but Jay and George knew I was steaming. When the crew told us there was a short delay before taping, I headed off to the ladies room to cool off and try to think of a clever way to deflect Stewart's version of acronym Jeopardy. When I jerked open the door to head back to the green room, I ran into Jay and George, stationed immediately outside the ladies room. "What the heck?" I barked as I slammed into them.

"We were afraid you might leave on us, ma'am," Rhynedance said. For the first time that day I laughed. And I survived the taping, probably because I did realize something as I headed onto the set. Something that everyone who does those programs should know: It's about the host, not you. Millions of people watch because they want *him* to be funny. And if that comes at your expense, that's okay. If you can take a good-natured punch and—even better—be self-deprecating, you will do just fine.

Not surprisingly, Secretary Rumsfeld was not completely sold on my late-night show strategy, and I didn't push it with him. And I didn't go out of my way to tell him about my appearance either. Near the end of my segment, Stewart very good-naturedly pressured me to acknowledge when we in the Pentagon had lied. "Does the Pentagon ever—and I know this probably never happens—lie?" Stewart said, getting a big laugh from the studio audience. "Do they ever lie? Are they lying? Answer me!"

"So far, only once that I know of," I answered (truthfully). "I saw Secretary Rumsfeld earlier this evening and he said, 'Where are you going?'"

My answer: "Nowhere sir!"

Q: A year ago I quit my entry-level job at the Justice Department to serve as press secretary for a congressional race in the northwest. My mother was horrified that I gave up a good job in D.C., but I really wanted campaign experience. Although we lost, it was a blast, and I made many friends. I really liked our candidate—he is smart, funny and in public service for all the right reasons. We enjoyed being in each other's company, and several times he said I was the best thing that ever happened to his staff. Near Election Day, some co-workers teased me that the boss was interested in me for more than poll numbers and that the spouse was getting twitchy. I laughed, told them they were nuts and chalked up their suspicions to sleep deprivation. But now I'm not so sure. The former candidate landed a plum assignment as EPA regional administrator, and his first move was to ask me if I want the top communications job. Relocating isn't the problem; worries about his romantic interests are. Should I say yes to the big job?

A: Wow. I know it's a tough job market, but I'd run for the hills on this one. Even if nothing developed between you two, you'd always wonder if you were hired for the wrong reasons.

What if you could have an adult conversation with him prior to taking the job? (And that's a big "if.") Of course he'll swear he only wants you on his team because of your professional assets. You take the job and then question everything—meetings, conversations, praise and criticism—through a prism of doubt. If he praises your work, you will worry it's because he has the hots for you. He dishes out some criticism, and you'll wonder if it's because you aren't willing to jump in bed with him. That's a poisonous way to work and live. Thank him for the offer, ask for a letter of recommendation (if he balks, you'll know what his real interest in you was) and get to work on your resume. There are good jobs out there with far fewer complications.

Q: Tweeting, texting and blogging have made the phrase "24/7 news cycle" seem ancient and painfully slow. Tens of thousands of policymakers, staff, and the journalists who cover them now engage in "real-time" analysis of political events. My boss is a four-term member of Congress from the Midwest who still reads his daily newspaper each morning (print version!) and is appalled by the media's emphasis on speed over substance. We're trying to drag him into the 21st century, but are so far unsuccessful. Can he be relevant if he's not on Facebook? Will any journalist take him seriously if he's not tweeting?

A: Politicians should be as connected and transparent as possible. More access is almost always a good thing. I worry, though, that social media, especially Twitter, encourages people to yack first and think later, and I share your boss's lament about fast over facts. The good news is the media you care about do sift through the clutter to find what matters.

"Journalists will take him seriously if he's a substantive member who does serious work," says NBC Justice and Supreme Court Correspondent Pete Williams. "The main event for reporters who cover Congress is what members actually do, rather than what they tweet.

"But this guy's boss is missing out on a way to keep in touch with the folks at home if he's not telling them what he's up to by using social media. One blast on Twitter can instantly inject a thought or a quote into the stream of news coverage. Some in Congress take to it naturally, some don't. If your boss is one who doesn't, you'll have to pick up the slack."

Andrea Mitchell says it's not a crucial decision for you or your boss. "To tweet or not to tweet!" she says. "Twitter is an enormously valuable source of information and amusement. I think of it as a tip sheet to stories or ideas I might want to explore. But I wouldn't worry if your boss isn't willing to live in the 140-character space. There are many players in Congress who don't. If they are smart, well-informed and play influential roles on big issues, they can ignore social media."

Andrea and Pete are saying that all the IT savvy in the world won't make up for a lack of substance. So don't try to force your square peg of a boss into a round hole of 21st century technology if it doesn't work for him. If it does, tweet prudently.

TURNS OUT MY JUDGMENT
IS ONLY RELIABLE 23/6.

CHAPTER SEVEN

BE WARY OF FAKE FRIENDS AND EMBRACE THE REALLY GOOD ONES

"My name is John Tower, and I don't."

Q: A friend wants me to speak at his liberal organization's conference, because they need a token Republican. I'm the only conservative he knows, and it doesn't hurt that I'm female. Do I do it even though some of my conservative friends will go nuts?

A: Do it! And if your conservative friends slam you, they are a) not really friends, and b) not very smart. If you believe in conservative principles and policies, you should feel comfortable pushing them in all environments, not just friendly ones. One of the best ways to learn about the opposition is to spend time with it. As one of the few Republicans willing to speak on college campuses (not always the friendliest of environments for conservatives), I seldom encounter a hostile crowd and am always happy I went. Okay, the University of Pittsburgh did have to hire extra security when I visited during the Iraq war, but nothing terrible happened. I show liberal professors that conservatives don't all have horns, and I hear what real young people are thinking, not just the mainstream media's take on American youth. (The occasional heckler is usually quickly shut down by the more reasonable members of your audience.)

You might be surprised at how nicely people respond when they see you've come into their lion's den. And if you keep your ears open, you just might learn something.

Q: Someone I considered a good friend took a job with a conservative think tank located near our favorite watering hole. She insists that I not come up to her office or even meet her out front when we're heading to happy hour. I'm slow, but finally figured out she didn't want her colleagues to know that she was friendly with someone from the other side of the aisle. Should I be hurt, angry or just let it go?

A: You should be hurt and pissed. Clearly your pal cares more about her reputation than your friendship. You need to think about what kind of friend she will be going forward. Good for occasional glasses of wine and a laugh or two? Absolutely. A friend you can call at 3 a.m. with a crisis? Maybe. A friend who will publicly defend you when you've made some major blunder at work and ended up in the news? Probably not.

Someone I considered a very good friend signed up with a liberal organization in town. I'm not as smart as you are, so it took me weeks to figure out why she repeatedly told me to call her cell or her direct line rather than the organization's main number. She didn't want her liberal friends to know she had a Republican friend. Nice. I was too much of a wimp to call her on it, so I let the insult fester for a long time, causing her no pain and bugging me a lot. I finally let it go. She's fun, and life's too short to drag that sort of emotional baggage along. I'm blessed with many good friends from both sides of the aisle, including my Democratic husband.

I guess the moral of the story is don't put all your friendship eggs in one basket, because some of them will break... and make her buy the drinks next time you're out together.

Q: Can Republicans and Democrats ever be friends? Can we return to the "old days," when Tip O'Neill and Ronald Reagan drank together and members of Congress from opposite sides of the aisle carpooled?

A: Of course. And they can be more than friends. (See: Husband, Mine...) Mary Matalin and James Carville are the most visible example of love trumping politics. My husband worked for then-Congressman Chuck Schumer, a liberal New York Democrat, and I worked for Senator John McCain, a conservative Arizona senator, when we first dated. I have plenty of Democratic friends, and Brian has plenty of Republican friends. The difference for us is that we care about a lot of things more than we care about someone's political stripes. That's not true for a lot of people, though. A really nice guy who bleeds "blue state" once told Brian he was sorry he and his wife couldn't have us over for dinner more often, but it was hard, what with, "Torie being a Republican and all."

Oh well. People like that miss out on some fascinating conversations.

Your second question taps into something more important. I roll my eyes when people moan and groan about how mean and tough Washington is these days. Puh-leez. Read any history of our government's early days—members of Congress beat each other with canes, presidential candidates paid for nasty lies to be printed about their opponents, and just about every politician was accused of having illegitimate children. Okay, so some things never change.

What has changed is that politicians see each other less and less in settings other than the House or Senate floor, an understandably partisan place. In the old days, Congressmen and their families lived in the Washington area, and the members went home for events and campaigning. Republicans and Democrats might disagree on issues, but their kids went to school together, their families socialized on weekends, and there were plenty of opportunities to grab a beer (as Reagan and O'Neill used to do). They saw—and valued—each other as people first, and politicians second.

Not any more. Now they spend as little time as possible in Washington, racing home for events and fundraising and seldom, if ever, engage those across the aisle in anything but partisan bickering.

There are exceptions. President George W. Bush and Senator Ted Kennedy joined forces on education reform. President Clinton worked with a Republican-led Congress to pass welfare reform. Senator John McCain and Senator John Kerry worked so closely on issues that rumors had Kerry as a potential VP candidate for John McCain when he ran for president in 2008. Republican New Jersey Governor Chris Christie embraced—figuratively and literally—President Obama for his help in the wake of Hurricane Sandy.

I know I sound like a Pollyanna on this, but I think we can all get along, to paraphrase Rodney King.

Q: My boss has known Anthony Weiner for 20 years. He feels sorry for him and worries about his family and wants to quietly make a few calls on his behalf. I'm completely opposed to the idea and have a hard time ginning up any sympathy for Weiner after what he did and how often he lied to his family, friends and colleagues. How can I tell my boss to back off? He says no one will know he's trying to help.

A: I'm with your boss, but he's kidding himself if he thinks he can do so quietly. Someone, somewhere will make sure the world knows he tried to help a serial sexter. If he's going to support Weiner, that's great. More kudos to your boss if he does so publicly, knowing it might hurt him politically.

Washington is a hotbed of Shakespearean tragedy themes. Every administration has numerous "et tu, Brute?" moments. The names change but the gory details are predictable.

"My name is John Tower, and I don't!"

That is how the diminutive ex-senator from Texas introduced himself at almost every speech. He cracked himself up, but the joke usually prompted uneasy laughs from people new to his material and groans from those who knew him well.

Bad joke aside, Tower was one of the Senate's most formidable defense and foreign policy experts. Back then, being a member of the "Tower Mafia" was an honor reserved for some of Washington's smartest guys—guys like Gary Hart and John McCain and Bill Cohen. They were Tower's students, devotees and brain trust.

Fast-forward to the first Bush Administration. President George H.W. Bush tapped Tower to be his Defense Secretary, a logical pick given Tower's background and easy relations with both sides of the aisle. We figured his confirmation would be a slam-dunk. Not.

Tower's nomination ran into trouble very quickly, and not because anyone questioned his defense credentials. They questioned his extra-curricular activities, many of which centered on women and vodka.

After a few weak "We support Senator Tower" statements, the Administration cooled on him. McCain was furious. "We'll do what the White House won't," he told his staff early one morning. "We'll rebut every bogus charge, we'll drum up support, we'll get this done." It sounded a little like "Come on, kids—let's put on a show!" and a lot more like, "Let's take a ride on the Titanic!"

It was just a matter of time before the White House pulled his nomination. McCain knew that, but he was going to fight anyway. Ignoring those who said supporting Tower was futile and could hurt him politically, McCain said, "I don't care. Sometimes, you just have to stick up for your friends."

I loved that and threw myself into our failed mission. We called reporters. We had friends send letters to the editors of major newspapers. We tried to energize military organizations, formal and informal. We did everything the White House legislative shop should have done.

The charges against Tower came in fast and furious and ridiculous. By today's standards, some of the accusations (e.g. he squeezed a female staffer's shoulder as he walked by her) seem quaint. Some were more serious.

It was exhausting. Back in Arizona, McCain would often call me first thing in the morning for the latest news on Tower. "You won't believe this one," I told him one morning, the exasperation at our wild goose chases in my voice. "Someone says Tower used to signal to Committee staffers that his drink needed to be refilled by putting the empty glass on his head! These people are really going too far!"

There was silence on the other end of the line. "Oh yeah," McCain finally said, trying hard not to laugh. "I remember that."

It went on for months. Near the end, we were working late on a Friday night, tackling the latest allegation. We needed to check something with Tower and couldn't find him. He wasn't answering his office phone, or his home phone. We got worried and finally had somebody *go* to his office and home just to make sure he hadn't, God forbid, killed himself. No Tower.

As the hours ticked by, we got closer and closer to missing the reporter deadlines that were so critical back then. Sitting alone in my office, staring at a phone that refused to ring with Tower on the other end, I had an idea. I pulled out a phone book and punched in a number.

"Jefferson Hotel," a distinguished voice answered.

"May I have the bar, please?" I asked politely. The front desk rang me through to the bar, where the bartender picked up immediately. In the background I heard piano music, men and women laughing and glasses clinking. It sounded like the fun part of *Casablanca*.

"Hello," I said. "This is Torie Clarke, and I'm calling from Senator John McCain's office. This is a crazy question, but by any chance is Senator Tower there?"

No way, I'm thinking, given everything we've been dealing with, would he be dumb enough to be in a bar—this bar—at a time like this.

"Why yes, ma'am, he's right here. Would you like to speak to him?"

He withdrew his nomination two weeks later.

Q: Can reporters and sources be friends? For example, does it help the working relationship if a reporter from the *Washington Post*, say, takes a Hill press secretary out for drinks and lunch occasionally, or does that cross some ethical boundary?

A: As the sly old put-down goes, some of my best friends are reporters. I find they are often bright, inquisitive, fun and, occasionally, royal pains in the rear. Of course, I could say the same about some relatives. I think a Hill press secretary should try hard to develop good working relationships and friendships might develop.

"Ethics rules are much tighter than they used to be," says NBC news correspondent Pete Williams, "and congressional staffers should be careful about accepting expensive meals or other favors from anyone, including reporters. But there's nothing wrong with the occasional lunch or after-work drink with a reporter."

Pete understands the relationship better than most—he covered politicians and was covered when he worked for Congressman and later Defense Secretary Dick Cheney.

"In fact, good reporters want to establish something more than a formal telephone-only relationship with the people they cover," he adds. "And yes, you may end up considering some reporters to be friends. But remember: their jobs come first. Just because you've become friendly will not stop that reporter from writing a negative story if your boss does something stupid. "

Andrea Mitchell agrees that reporters and sources can be friends, "as long as they understand the ground rules of each conversation. Washington can often seem like a small town, so there are occasions when someone who is a friend suddenly gets appointed to a government job and becomes a potential source. In that case, it's best to establish the rules of the road immediately so that both you and the new government official are protected from any suggestion of improper contact."

She thinks it's fine for a reporter and press secretary to have lunch or drinks, "assuming they split the check. Social conversations can help provide context and depth to a reporter's understanding of a complex issue. Many foreign policy discussions take place over dinner or drinks at embassies.

"Reporters have to be careful, however, not to permit friendship or social acquaintance to inhibit aggressive reporting when and if that becomes necessary."

In other words, as Joyce Rumsfeld says, "Remember that you have your job to do, and they have their job to do."

CHAPTER EIGHT

HOW TO CONTROL YOUR TEMPER
AND HOW TO LOSE IT

"Don't Get Mad—Get Franken"

Q: As a frequent State Department briefer, I get lots of unsolicited advice from people who think they're more qualified to do my job. "You should have said it this way..." "Did you think about the audience in (Your Small and Remote Country Here)?" I'd like to tell them all to pound sand, but I'd also like to keep my job.

A: Every single place I've worked I've encountered legislative assistants, lawyers, policy wonks and even interns who thought briefing the media—on the record or on background—was part of their job. And I've found that the people who were worst at *their* jobs spent the most time trying to do mine.

Give most of your helpful advisors a non-committal "Hmm, that's an interesting way of looking at it" when they make a moronic comment. Occasionally, you do have to listen to criticism—if the Secretary of State says you screwed up, you probably did and should start groveling.

I never watched my Pentagon briefings. It was hard enough getting through them; the thought of re-living them hours later was more than I could stomach. I should have for lots of reasons, not the least of which was that I could have improved my performances. I justified not watching by telling myself—and others—that I was too busy doing important work to go back and watch something that had happened hours before.

Somehow, though, Rumsfeld found the time. Often I'd arrive at work early in the morning to find a newly fallen snowflake waiting for me. "You need to pause when you move from one topic to another," Rumsfeld cautioned in one. "Talking about soldiers killed in action deserves a very different approach than upcoming combat action," he correctly pointed out.

Sometimes the critiques were more immediate and significant. In the fall of 2001, I was briefing with one of the several military people the Joint Staff teamed up with me. In general, I would handle policy matters and the broader national security issues; my counterpart would handle the finer details of the military actions underway. Given the pressure of the times and high-stakes nature of our comments, I developed quite a bond with my fellow briefers, together in an information foxhole, so to speak.

The overwhelming majority of the briefers did an exceptional job. Every word did matter, though, and sometimes mistakes were made, including by me. Once, my military counterpart acknowledged the ferociousness with which some Al Qaeda were defending their turf in Afghanistan. "Yeah," he mused (musing is seldom a good idea in a Pentagon briefing), "they did turn out to be tougher than we expected."

I didn't say "Oops!" but I did think that might not go down well in some quarters.

No kidding. By the time I got back to my office there was a

message telling me to head up to Rumsfeld's office. "Geez," I fumed
to myself. "I barely have time to *do* the briefings; how does he have
time to watch them?"

Sure enough, Rumsfeld swung around from his stand-up desk
as I entered and pointed a finger at me. "Your guy blew it today.
What the heck was he thinking when he praised Al Qaeda? The last
thing we need right now is to pump them up and simultaneously
demoralize our troops!" As the head of all things communication at
the Pentagon, I was responsible for what military and civilians alike
said at that podium.

A large part of me knew Rumsfeld was right, but another part
of me thought (maybe hoped) that he was overstating the impact.
It was one line out of dozens. Besides, you have to stick up for your
foxhole buddy.

"I don't agree," I said. "He made it very clear how well our guys
are doing, and I doubt his one line is going to have much of an
impact beyond this building."

"You're wrong," Rumsfeld barked.

We went back and forth for a few minutes, neither giving ground.

A few days later, the SecDef and I were thousands of miles
from Washington, swinging through several countries to shore
up support for our military actions in Afghanistan. High on the
list was a visit to Islamabad and meetings with Pakistan President
Pervez Musharraf. In less than 24 hours on the ground there would
be several meetings (only the one in which Musharraf and Rumsfeld
met one-on-one was important) and a dinner in Rumsfeld's honor.

Whenever we did dinners, I tried to seat myself so I had one eye
on Rumsfeld in case he needed anything. He seldom did. On this
night, though, he gestured to me about halfway through dinner to
come over to his table. Musharraf was on his right, so I was mentally

ticking through the things Rumsfeld might ask about – the next
day's press conference, for instance.

When I leaned down toward them, Rumsfeld said with a big
smile, "President Musharraf has something he wants to tell you."

"How great is this," I thought. "The president of Pakistan wants
to talk to me." I didn't high-five myself, but I was tempted.

"Your fellow briefer said things very badly the other day,"
Musharraf said solemnly. "That was a very good day for the Taliban,
and a very bad day for our friends who are fighting there. You need
to know that everyone watches those briefings."

"Yes sir," was all I could say.

"That's all," Rumsfeld said, and I crawled back to my seat. When
I got back to my table, I had just one thought: "I hate CNN!"

**Q: I work for the very ambitious head of a small federal agency who
truly believes she'll run Treasury some day. (She is, in my opinion,
delusional.) Her motto seems to be "ignore and attack"—ignore all
criticism and attack those who dare to challenge her on issues large
or small. Her enemies list is longer than the Oxford English Dictionary.
How can we help her realize that constructive criticism is a good thing?
We need as much help as we can get moving this agency's agenda
forward, and we won't get there if she refuses to listen to anyone.**

A: Appeal to her vanity. All successful leaders have kitchen cabinets,
unofficial advisors who can bring important facts and context. The
strongest (and often most successful) politicians are those willing
to embrace those who oppose them. As Doris Kearns Goodwin's
remarkable book *Team of Rivals* made clear, Lincoln knew the
many challenges he faced as he entered the White House would
only be overcome by bringing former enemies into his camp.
President Reagan hired James Baker, campaign manager for his

primary opponent, as his White House Chief of Staff. President Obama kept Robert Gates, a Bush '43 appointee, as his Secretary of Defense and tapped Ray LaHood, former Republican Member of Congress from Illinois, as his Secretary of Transportation.

To get where she is, your boss must be hard-working, and have little tolerance for inefficiency. Tell her that attacking every critic is a waste of time and energy, and accomplishes little.

It will be hard for her to hear this (and for you to say it), but there are a lot of brilliant people in this town, so having the courage and smarts to correctly process criticism can be a very smart strategy, and a good way to win the long game.

Q: Help! I am a digital junkie! After 10- or even 12-hour days on the Hill, I will obsessively check Twitter, Facebook and multiple political sites for mentions of my boss. I often engage in online exchanges (many of them unpleasant ones at 2:30 in the morning), eager to battle anyone who dares to criticize him. Too often I regret my comments the next day.

A: I admire your loyalty and question your sanity. And health. As my friend Dan says, "Nothing good happens between midnight and 5:00 a.m.!"

A *USA Today* reporter once asked Andy Rosenthal of the *New York Times* about me for a profile when I was working on a campaign. Andy probably said some nice things about me, but what ended up in the piece about my skills as a press secretary was, "Well, she hasn't lied to me yet." If you know Andy, that's actually a compliment. I should have known that then, but in my sleep-deprived state, I flipped, and fumed to everyone within 10 miles. Not surprisingly, my stupid remarks got back to Andy, which started a silly kerfuffle that took a couple of days to unwind. A day or two that would have been better spent on more meaningful matters, by the way.

So here's my advice: Go to bed! You're doing no one any good at 3 a.m., and your obsession and snarky comments are hurting you and your boss. Unless someone has accused your boss of a felony, chances are any tweet can wait until you've had some sleep. If not, take a deep breath, then call someone you trust for an honest take on it. Chances are, your "lifeline" will wisely tell you to cool off, and walk away from the temptation to prove your boss has a thin-skinned Twitter nut working for him.

Q: A reporter got some facts wrong in a piece that was highly critical of me. My staff says I should leave it alone. I get it—we don't want to draw more attention to a hatchet job, but I hate to let him get away with sloppy reporting. Should I call his boss, tweet about it or shut up?

A: It sounds like you hired a pretty good staff. Listen to them. It seldom, if ever, pays for a politician to get in a fight with reporters.

If the reporter got important facts wrong, your press secretary should do something. But did the reporter say you wore an ugly yellow tie? Don't ask for a correction. But if he wrote that you supported funding rebels in Syria when you're opposed to U.S. involvement there, then have your press secretary quietly and calmly talk with the reporter's editor. You stay out of it. Whatever you do, do not accost the reporter in person or on the phone.

Long ago, Anne Q. Hoy covered John McCain and the Arizona Congressional delegation for the *Arizona Republic*. She worked hard and conscientiously. One day she had a front-page piece that for some reason infuriated John. He ranted to me. He raved to others on the staff. He complained to friends on the phone. And then, despite my begging, he called Anne's boss to blast her. About two minutes after John hung up, very pleased with himself, Anne called me. She was happy, too. "Please, please, *please* have John call my boss as much as he wants," she said. "I just got a raise!"

Q: A very talented advance guy deserted our campaign months ago. His candidate flamed out, and now he wants to return. I say no way we take the traitor back. As a matter of fact, I think we should put the word out that no one in the party should hire this guy. You can't let disloyal behavior like that go unpunished, right?

A: I admire your principles, but I have a question for you: Is he an exceptionally good advance man, and do you need another one? Did he provide the campaign to which he ran inside information that shouldn't have been shared? If not, what's the harm?

I think you should let it go, and get on with the more pressing matters of your campaign. Even if you wanted to ruin his life, do you really have time for that? If the answer is "yes," you're not working hard enough at your real job.

Choose your fights carefully. Washington is a small town, and if you stick around long enough you'll bump into the same people, again and again. Why burn bridges unless absolutely necessary? In the city that invented dogs as pets (because if you want a friend in this town...), it's always tempting to whack those who have wronged you, but save your bullets.

I work hard to keep my occasionally short temper in check, and my eagerness to apologize quickly for a burst of temper has saved me many times. At the National Cable and Television Association I would deliver apologies along with a nice bottle of wine. Dan Brenner, the general counsel there, once begged me to argue with him because he loved the wine.

On the other hand, the perfect bit of revenge can be exhilarating...

When you hang around D.C. as long as I have, you get to know many of the network producers and bookers. If you're humane, you have sympathy for them. They work for demanding, often unreasonable bosses, and have to deal with rapidly changing events, last-minute cancellations by guests and a general ambiance of chaos. Katherine O'Hearn is a pro's pro in that business, and I have dealt with her for years. When I was at the Pentagon, she often asked me to appear on Tina Brown's short-lived CNBC show *Topic [A] with Tina Brown*, which taped in New York. Fortunately, I was able to answer that my busy schedule kept me from flying up. I had no interest in doing the show and was always glad I had an excuse. I never asked, but my gut told me that Katherine and Tina probably felt a little pressure to occasionally have a Republican on the show.

When I left the Pentagon, it got harder to turn her down. "Please, please come to New York," Katherine begged me one day. "Tina loves you and is dying to talk about the embedded media." Despite serious doubts that Tina loved me, I agreed.

A few days before the taping, Katherine told me Tina wanted to add a journalist to our conversation. "To get their view of embedding," she said. Fine, I thought, knowing they would probably pick a journalist who A) was not embedded during the Iraq War; and B) was cranky about embedding. Bingo! They asked Christiane Amanpour. She's a first-rate journalist, and I really didn't mind, but since the original pitch of the show was changing, I was getting a little cranky.

The night before I was to fly to New York, Katherine called again. "Hey, I know you won't mind, but we're adding Al Franken to the show tomorrow—it'll be great!" As everyone well knows, whether you agree or disagree with Al Franken, when he wants something he usually gets it. Be a successful comedian? Check. Write a best-selling book? Check. Get elected to the U.S. Senate? Check. His take-no-prisoners attitude clearly played a large part in his success, even if it aggravates many of the people trapped in his orbit.

Now I was officially cranky. What went through my mind was,

"He's a nut. He's a media hog. He's really funny! He knows the more outrageous he is, the more attention he's going to get. This will be awful." But all I said to Katherine was, "He's got a new book out, so that's all we'll talk about!"

"No, no, no," Katherine said. "Tina will not let him monopolize the taping!"

The next morning I flew to New York. Christiane and I got to the studio at the same time and headed to makeup. Franken was not there. "He's running a little late," squeaked the 12-year-old intern Katherine sent to give us the update, "but he's on his way." We waited 10, 15, 30 minutes and no Franken. About 45 minutes late, he strolls in, high-fiving staff and crew, 10 copies of his new book under his arm.

When we finally sat down on the set with Tina, things went south fast. Franken knows how to steer an audience, even if it was just the three of us. Any topic Tina tried to raise—Iraq, the media or the President—he tied it to something in his book. He even gave page numbers as he connected every world event to something he had written. I found myself alternating between, "I'm gonna kill him!" and "Damn, he's good at this!"

Every once in a while, Christiane and I tried to get a word in, but his loud voice and rapid page-turning drowned us out. Unable to control myself any longer, I leaned forward in my chair during a break, pointed my finger at Tina and yelled, "Are you going to take control of this show or what?"

The answer was "what," because we rambled along on the Franken Express for another 10 minutes. When it was finally over, I could not get out of there fast enough. Jerking the mike from my lapel, I quickly and disingenuously thanked Tina and Christiane and headed for the door.

Katherine ran after me. "Don't worry, Torie! We know he got a little out of control, but we're going to edit that way down!" Mad at him, mad at Katherine and Tina, and mostly mad at myself for agreeing to do the show, I said through clenched teeth, "Good luck with that!" and headed out the door.

"Damn!" I said to no one when I hit the sidewalk. It was raining, traffic was awful and I knew I'd never get a cab. "What a (expletive-deleted) day!"

As I peered up and down the street, vainly looking for an empty cab, a shiny black limo rolled up. The window slides down, and the driver in a black cap says, "Franken?"

For a split second, I did nothing. Then I said "Yep," and hopped in the back. And in about five seconds, all the anger and frustration I had been feeling disappeared. "I have Al Franken's limo. How great is this?" I was giddy.

Not only did I steal his car, I kept it for the afternoon. I called some friends and we spent the rest of the day getting lunch and doing a little shopping before I headed back to the airport.

ET TU, FIDO?

ACKNOWLEDGMENTS

In most Washington books this would be the longest section. The author, desperately seeking to flatter all and to insult none, lists person after person. Most of those named have little—if any—relevance to the book itself. In a blow for simplicity and honesty, here are my heartfelt thanks to those who made "Surviving" a reality.

First, last and always: Brian, Colin, Devan and Charlie—the best of friends, most honest of critics and fiercest of protectors.

Lewis Black: Genius

Barbara Feinman Todd: Consigliere

Nick Galifianakis: Inspirer

Debbie Weil: Publisher

And thanks to everyone else who has ever made my career(s) fun, challenging, educational, rewarding, scary and meaningful.

Any mistakes in this book—and I am sure there are some—are my fault.Please don't blame them on the people named above.

ABOUT THE AUTHOR

Torie Clarke is Senior Vice President for Global Corporate Affairs for SAP, a leading multinational software company. Clarke has served in three Administrations, most recently as Assistant Secretary of Defense under Donald Rumsfeld. She is recognized in the private and public sectors as an expert on communications in the age of transparency.

Prior to SAP, Clarke was a Senior Adviser to Comcast NBC Universal, ran the Washington office of Hill & Knowlton, served as Vice President of the National Cable Television Association and was Press Secretary to Senator John McCain. She is the author of *Lipstick on a Pig: Winning in the No-Spin Era by Someone Who Knows the Game.*

Clarke serves on the Senior Advisory Committee of Harvard's Institute of Politics and is on the Board of Trustees of the Potomac School. She and her husband, Brian Graham, live in Chevy Chase, Maryland with their three children.

Visit survivorwashington.com.
Reach Torie at torie@survivorwashington.com or follow her on Twitter @survivordcbook.com.

ABOUT THE ILLUSTRATOR

Nick Galifianakis is an award-winning cartoonist whose nationally syndicated work is recognized alongside the must-read advice column by Carolyn Hax, named by Time magazine as America's best advice column. Nick is the author of *If You Loved Me, You'd Think This Was Cute: Uncomfortably True Cartoons About You*, a collection of his cartoons.

Visit nick at nickandzuzu.com.
Follow Nick on Twitter @ngalifianakis.

CPSIA information can be obtained at www.ICGtesting.com
Printed in the USA
BVOW01*1804240914

368200BV00004B/6/P